The Power of
Thought

Messages and Thoughts Celebrating the Life of
Dr. Martin Luther King Jr.

DR. WRIGHT L. LASSITER JR.

Order this book online at www.trafford.com
or email orders@trafford.com

Most Trafford titles are also available at major online book retailers.

Printed in the United States of America.

ISBN: 978-1-4269-9589-7 (sc)
ISBN: 978-1-4269-9590-3 (hc)
ISBN: 978-1-4269-9591-0 (e)

Library of Congress Control Number: 2011916814

Trafford rev. 09/20/2011

 www.trafford.com

North America & international
toll-free: 1 888 232 4444 (USA & Canada)
phone: 250 383 6864 ✦ fax: 812 355 4082

CONTENTS

PART FOUR
Supporting Messages

PART FIVE
End Notes

PART ONE
The Setting For The Messages

DEDICATION

This collection of messages by the author, with the inclusion of selected articles by other journalists, is dedicated to the memory of my father and mother, Dr. Wright L. Lassiter, Sr. and Mrs. Ethel Franklin Lassiter. It was through the guidance, nurture, and teachings that I was prepared to live and advance in the segregated South. They taught me how to survive and advance, in spite of the limitations imposed by Jim Crow laws and practices in our hometown of Vicksburg, Mississippi, and conversely throughout the South during a very difficult period in the life of this nation.

It is further dedicated to my late younger brother, Dr. Lewis Leon Lassiter, who preached the gospel and taught others using themes articulated by Dr. Martin Luther King, Jr., during his lifetime.

It is finally dedicated to a younger brother, Colonel Albert E. Lassiter, who braved the segregationist forces in Jackson, Mississippi as a student at Tougaloo College. He bravely joined with other students from that private, historically black college, when they held sit-in demonstrations at lunch counters in Jackson, and also experienced difficulties from law enforcement officers that resulted in their being jailed.

FOREWORD

The contents of this publication represents a project that I started and stopped on several occasions as other projects emerged with a higher priority. However, each time that I have been asked to speak at the annual observance of the Dr. Martin Luther King, Jr. national holiday, my thoughts returned to this unfinished work.

For the past two years I have been a part of the doctoral faculty from Dallas Baptist University that engages in an intensive week of study and exploration called "The Washington Experience." We spend a week in Washington and for each of the prior periods we have devoted time to engage in research and dialogue on important figures that have shaped this nation. The three figures that we have studied each year were Washington, Lincoln and King.

As we concluded our preparations for the 2008 "Washington Experience," I was given the assignment to present one of the opening lectures on the life of Dr. Martin Luther King, Jr. Having received that assignment, it seemed apropos that I should bring closure to this long-delayed project and have a product to share with the doctoral students and faculty. As all writers will acknowledge, incidents and circumstances can serve as the catalyst or stimulus to move a project to completion.

Because I was caused to live through all of the social periods of this nation (with the exception of the Depression Era), I found utility in sharing with audiences episodes and anecdotes that I considered relevant whenever I was asked to deliver an address commemorating the work and life of Dr. Martin Luther King, Jr.

I was privileged to be working at Tuskegee Institute (Alabama) and had the opportunity to observe the Montgomery Bus Boycott first-hand. It is not often that one can be a part of what I would call "living history." From the time of the Montgomery Bus Boycott until the time of the assassination of Dr. King, I was privileged to be both an observer and a participant in the making of history as a result of the courageous work of Dr. King.

Two examples in 1965 of my personal involvement in the social change movement in this nation are instructive.

My family and I were returning to Tuskegee from a vacation visit with long-time friends in Baltimore, Maryland by car. My family consisted of my wife and two children under age 5. As there were no motels or hotels available to Negroes at that time, I was trying to drive straight-through. Upon arriving in Rome, Georgia it was clear to me that it would be dangerous for me to try to continue driving. Subjecting my family to the ordeal of sleeping in a cramped car was not inviting. I told my wife that the Civil Rights Act of 1965 had been passed and was now the law of the land. The piece of legislation made public accommodations available to all citizens, regardless of race. I told my wife that this was a time to test the power of the law. My wife was nervous and distraught for challenging segregation laws had proven to be dangerous. Nevertheless, I told her that all they could do was refuse to give us accommodations.

I went through the front door of the Rome (Georgia) Hotel and moved to the registration counter and indicated that I needed a room for me and my family (wife and two children). We were traveling from Baltimore, Maryland to our home in Tuskegee, Alabama and I was too tired to drive any longer. Without any hesitation, I was given the registration card and we were given a room large enough for a double bed and two baby cribs.

Upon returning to our car, my wife was wide-eyed and nervous, but relieved when I told her that "all was well, we were registered!" I parked our car "in the front," and took my family and our belongings up to our hotel room. Obviously there were some stares, but only out of curiosity.

The next morning my wife (who now had her own brand of courage) called to the front desk and asked if an iron and ironing board was available. Within ten minutes someone was knocking on the door with both.

When everyone was dressed, we packed and went down to the restaurant, through the regular front door, to have breakfast. The white waitress treated us with the utmost courtesy. As we waited for our order, we noticed that all of the kitchen staff (all were Negroes) just standing in the kitchen-area door looking at us—and smiling. You see, we were the first Negroes to ever received accommodations at the Rome Hotel.

The second incident was my being appointed to the Board of Commissioners of the Tuskegee Housing Authority, and having had thrust upon me the implementation of the Civil Rights Act of 1965 as relates to public housing. I had to convert the formerly all-white staff of the housing authority, and the housing developments into an integrated entity.

Eight years later when my tenure on the Board of Commissioners ended, the Tuskegee Housing Authority had gained national stature for its advances in providing equal-opportunity housing for low-income citizens. The Tuskegee Housing Authority was one of the first in the nation to introduce the ownership option for residents of the Housing Authority.

Why do I mention these two personal incidents? They are noteworthy because it was the efforts of Dr. King that provided the stimulus for the passage of legislation that enabled persons of color to be treated fairly in this nation.

Thus, the words that are reflected in this selected collection of speeches by me were deeply influenced by Dr. King and also by the circumstances of the times that I lived in.

THE AMERICAN DREAM

It is found in those majestic words of the Declaration of Independence, words lifted to cosmic proportions. "We hold these truths to be self-evident, that all men are created equal, that they are endowed by God, Creator, with certain inalienable Rights, that among those are Life, Liberty, and the pursuit of Happiness." This is a dream. It's a great dream.

If we are going to make the American dream a reality, we are challenged to work in an action program to get rid of the last vestiges of segregation and discrimination. This problem isn't going to solve itself, however much people tell us this.

We have a great dream. It started way back in 1776, and God grant that America will be true to her dream.

I still have a dream this morning: one day all of God's black children will be respected like his white children.

I still have a dream this morning that one day the lion and the lamb will lie down together, and every man will sit under his own vine and fig tree and none shall be afraid.

I still have a dream this morning that one day all men everywhere will recognize that out of one blood God made all men to dwell upon the face of the earth.

I still have a dream this morning that one day every valley shall be exalted, and every mountain and hill will be made low; the rough places will be made plain, and the crooked places straight; and the glory of the Lord shall be revealed, and all flesh shall see it together.

I still have a dream this morning that truth will reign supreme and all of God's children will respect the dignity and worth of human personality. And when this day comes the morning stars will sing together and the sons of God will shout for joy.

"We hold these truths to be self-evident that all men are created equal, that they are endowed by their Creator with certain inalienable Rights, that among these are Life, Liberty, and the pursuit of Happiness."

Dr. Martin Luther King, Jr.
Delivered at Ebenezer Baptist Church
Atlanta, Georgia
July 4, 1965

PART TWO
The King Biography

TELLING THE STORIES

I have a significant number of clippings in my MLK file in my home office. All of them feature editorial writers and syndicated reporters who share their thoughts about Dr. King and the national holiday each year. An assortment of views written by these individuals is included in this assemblage of materials to underscore the need to continue pursuing the "dream," and that "we are not there yet."

All of them make the point that we cannot forget the past, nor can we let icons like Martin Luther King, Jr. come to become nothing more than mere historical footnotes.

Jim Mitchell, an editorial writer for the Dallas Morning News wrote that "Americans must learn racial dialogue for the sake of healing." He continues, "For all the great opportunities this country offers, its history of slavery and racial discrimination has created memories that can't be forgotten. Being black in America isn't a temporal moment that allows you to kick off the ugly moments of the past like a pair of hot, sweaty work boots. There are too many reminders, none can be completely erased."

DR. MARTIN LUTHER KING, JR.
HIS LIFE IN BRIEF

Life began for Martin Luther King, Jr. on January 15, 1929, in Atlanta, Georgia. The son of a militant Atlanta minister, he grew up with the spirit of social protest around him. His grandfather was one of Georgia's first NAACP leaders and helped organize a boycott against newspapers that had disparaged Black voters. His father was also in the forefront of civil rights battles aimed at securing equal rights for Blacks in America.

Dr. King was raised in the warmth of a tightly knit family, where the virtues of good family life were emphasized. He developed from his earliest years a keen sensitivity over the unfair treatment given Blacks in the South.

Dr. King, a bright student, entered Atlanta's Morehouse College at only fifteen years of age. After graduating, he attended Crozier Theological Seminary in Chester, Pennsylvania, and later Boston University where he earned his doctorate degree in 1955. While in college, Dr. King had been influenced by India's Mahatma Gandhi whose philosophy of non-violence and passive resistance helped to bring about freedom for the people of India.

Dr. King began his Christian ministry in Montgomery, Alabama at the Dexter Avenue Baptist Church in May of 1954. A year and a half later, the eyes of the world focused on the young

14

minister as he led a successful boycott against segregation on that city's public buses.

The boycott began on December 1, 1955, when Mrs. Rosa Parks, a Black seamstress, who refused to surrender her seat to a white man, was arrested and fined. In response, the Black community called for a boycott of Montgomery's transit line, and Martin Luther King, Jr. was elected to lead the movement. The boycott lasted 381 days. During that time, Dr. King courageously guided his supporters despite intense opposition. Finally, the U.S. Supreme Court ruled that bus segregation was illegal. Dr. King won a great victory using peaceful techniques, thus heralding a new period of agitation for Black equality.

To continue the work begun in Montgomery, Dr. King formed the Southern Christian Leadership Conference in 1957, an organization committed to non-violent direct action. Soon, Dr. King and the SCLC became active participants in the student led sit-ins of the early sixties.

After a civil rights movement in Albany, Georgia met with only partial success, Dr. King re-grouped his forces for a massive attack on segregation in Birmingham, Alabama. The movement touched off a powder keg of racial hatred and resentment. Police Chief Eugene "Bull" Connor countered the civil rights demonstrators with fire hoses, clubs and dogs. Extremists added beatings, murders and bombings. Citizens were shocked as the world press front-paged these outrageous incidents. A new wave of unity among Blacks sparked sit-ins, demonstrations and marches throughout the U.S.

The climax to the events in Birmingham—which had proved that non-violent action could triumph—was the March on Washington. On August 28, 1963, the greatest civil rights demonstration the country had ever seen took place. More than 200,000 people, White and Black, came from every part of the

United States and joined together in a demonstration for justice, equality of opportunity and economic opportunity. The inspiration of this huge gathering was Dr. King's famous "I Have a Dream" speech. He spoke these immortal words:

"I have a dream that one day this nation will rise up and live out the true meaning of its creed: 'We hold these truths to be self-evident that all men are created equal.'"

Less than three weeks after the March on Washington, a bomb killed four little Black girls in a Birmingham church. Dr. King and the Black community faced an agonizing test in maintaining a non-violent spirit.

In the spring of 1964, a massive demonstration took place in St. Augustine, Florida and Dr. King was arrested again. Before the demonstration ended, President Lyndon Johnson signed the Civil Rights Act of 1964.

In 1964, Dr. King was awarded the Nobel Peace Prize, the second American Black (Dr. Ralph Bunche was the first) to win it. He gave the entire $54,000 cash award to the Southern Christian Leadership Conference and other organizations for a fund for education in non-violence.

In 1965, the drive for voter registration in Selma, Alabama ignited several violent attacks upon Dr. King's forces by police and ruffians. Civil rights demonstrators were clubbed, tear-gassed, and bullwhipped. Several marchers were murdered. Dr. Martin Luther King staunchly refused to halt his drive despite the violence. Eventually the patient, persistent pressure of non-violent action won out and Dr. King triumphantly led his marchers from Selma to Montgomery.

In the summer of 1966, Congress enacted, and President Johnson signed the most extensive voting legislation in history. In a few years the Black vote doubled in the South and thousands of Black officials were elected to public office.

When the violence and destruction erupted in the ghettos of America's cities, Dr. King showed his great strength of character. Unswervingly, he reaffirmed his dedication to non-violence and continued to struggle to see liberty and justice reign in America.

In New York in April 1967, Dr. King led 125,000 anti-war demonstrators from Central Park to the United Nations. Here he told the crowd, "Great moral issues are indissoluble. In my case, I've been preaching non-violence for years. Wouldn't it be inconsistent for me not speak out against the war in Vietnam?"

Late in March 1968, Dr. King journeyed to Memphis, Tennessee to assist striking sanitation workers. His first march, however, ended in rioting and looting. Assured by his advisors that violence could be prevented in subsequent demonstrations, the Black leader agreed to plan another march. After one of the planning sessions, Dr. King, on the balcony of his motel room chatted with some of his aides. The crack of a rifle shoot broke the conversation. Martin Luther King, Jr. lay dead.

On April 9, 1968, the funeral service for Dr. King took place in Atlanta at his home church, the Ebenezer Baptist Church. People of goodwill throughout the world mourned his untimely death.

Note #1—Presented at the Dallas Independent School District's Martin Luther King Jr. Memorial Tribute—Where Do We Go from Here? Nonviolence: A Blueprint for Life—January 15, 1992—El Centro College—Dallas, Texas.

Note #2—The author was associated with Tuskegee Institute in Tuskegee, Alabama during the time of the Montgomery Bus Boycott, and all of the Alabama demonstrations and incidents cited in this historical summary.

THE LEGACY OF MARTIN LUTHER KING, JR.

Each January the nations pays tribute to Martin Luther King, Jr., an American hero. The King holiday provides an occasion for us to reaffirm our commitment to his dream for America. We gain strength from his courage on so many battlefields—from the beginning in Montgomery, Alabama in 1955 to the end in Memphis in 1968.

We could honor his memory in a thousand ways. I choose to honor him for the political legacy he gave to the disadvantaged and disenfranchised in America. It is especially important at this annual memorial to remind ourselves of this legacy.

His legacy challenges each of us to use the power of politics and public office to pursue equal justice, due process of law, and true liberation for all Americans. It challenges us to believe—as he did—that "Injustice anywhere is a threat to justice everywhere," and that "we are caught in an inescapable network of mutuality tied in a single garment of destiny."

What King knew, as did others before him, was that in America political participation is the shortest road to power sharing and to improving the human condition. Law has its limits. Moral suasion has its limits. But politics endures so long as we profess to be a democratic society.

He said in 1967, "for years I labored with the idea of reforming the existing institutions of the society, a little change here, a little change there. Now I feel differently. I think you've got to have a reconstruction of the entire society, a revolution of values."

This nonviolent revolution must rely on direct political action. Clearly, this was the path that King envisioned in his call for a new thrust "powerful enough, dramatic enough, morally appealing enough, so that people of good will, the churches, labor, liberals, intellectuals, students, poor people themselves would begin to put pressure on Congressmen to achieve goals of a just society. As one author put it, "racial compassion had to be reinforced by old-fashioned American political quid pro quo."

Martin Luther King, Jr. gave focus and leadership to black American's struggle for political empowerment. The cause may have been education, eradication of hunger, jobs, or the right to eat at a restaurant, or take any seat on a bus, but the objective was always the same. To achieve equality and justice, to be heard, to be taken seriously, to be respected; to sit in the legislative and executive chambers and take part in decisions on who gets what, when, and how in our society.

Just before he died, Dr. King saw his dream beginning to become reality. Street politics moved indoors—into Congress, into state houses, into city halls. And today there are more than 8,500 black elected officials representing many millions of Americans. Their presence assures us that the civil rights movement is not dead. It is marching to the best of different drummers. Its leaders are sitting-in at city halls, state legislatures, and the U.S. Congress. They are marching into executive offices. They are challenging the political systems with their ideas.

So, on what would have been Dr. King's 70th birthday, we are thankful for his victories on so many battlefields: public accommodations, voting rights, equal employment opportunity.

We are fired by his inspiration, his sermons of love and hope. We continue to share his dream that one day all of the "sons of former slaves and sons of former slave owners will be able to sit down together at the table of brotherhood," and that "little black boys and black girls will be able to join hands with little white boys and white girls as sisters and brothers."

Our task is to uphold the legacy of Dr. Martin Luther King, Jr. by continuing the battle and the journey that he fought so valiantly for.

Long live the memory of Dr. Martin Luther King, Jr.

MARTIN LUTHER KING, JR.: A LIFE OF DEPTH AND INTEGRITY

Martin Luther King, Jr. was a man of deep, uncompromising faith. This was shown in his radical commitment to pacifism and peaceful protest and in his call for racial and class reconciliation. He called for justice and righteous living from the people of God. His famous "Dream" speech fused the vision of a better world predicted by the gospel, with the contemporary social conditions he sought to change. His faith challenged the separation between the sacred and secular in the church of his day. He sought to preach and live a holistic gospel that engaged the full needs of humankind with the fullness of the good news of God.

As a direct result of his burning faith, King was a man of action. He took seriously the mandate of Jesus announced in the Sermon on the Mount. He blessed those who were actually peace "makers," which by definition requires not just prayer, but action. "We must learn that to expect God to do everything while we do nothing is not faith but superstition," King said. His faith in this context demanded more than just political rhetoric and theological semantics. This led to the many peaceful protests that were to rock the American establishment and give rise to some of the most brutal and racist attacks in the history of the American civil rights movement.

The true power of King was to meet brutality, bigotry and hate with the weapons of compassion, forgiveness and love. "Love is the only force capable of transforming an enemy into a friend," he said.

Some of King's harshest words and challenges were addressed, not to members of the Ku Klux Klan or racists, but to the people of God. "This generation will not be judged for the evil the bad people have done, but for the appalling silence of the good," he said. King thought that Christians condoned the injustice and oppression that characterized race relations in this country in the 1960s by their silence. He urged them to take up the gospel's prophetic mantle and speak for truth and justice in a vacuum of prejudice.

King called unrelentingly for God's people to speak as God would speak, live as God would have them live, and to be active instruments of change.

King was also a man of deep, sacrificial commitment. He held up the awesome call of the gospel as something to which people could give their all. In talking about the purpose of people's lives he stated: "A man who won't die for something is not fit to live." This all-or-nothing challenge was at the very heart of King's philosophy of life and theology. He lifted up the dream of a new world as something possible and achievable by people willing to pay the price. He knew it would cost him dearly, but he embraced it as a disciple of Christ.

King, like so many, is in danger of being viewed as a stained glass window, a symbol detached from the power of his life and work. He was no perfect preacher. Most biblical heroes wrestled with human weaknesses and in the midst of that wrestling, sought to live out to the full their calling from God. Certainly King struggled in this way.

Like him, we need to be people of faith. An army of faith marching on its knees—secure enough in our faith to ask difficult questions and wrestle with the nightmares of our world. We must hold forth the absolutes of truth and love in a society that is so often filled with confusion and bitterness. To live lives of depth and integrity in the face of shallowness and compromise. To light up a beacon of faith in a dark, dark world.

King challenges us to be people of action. Jesus' Great Commission will not be fulfilled by a superficial war of words and theological pronouncements. In modeling the heart of King and proclaiming the truth of Scripture, we need to live lives that reflect the radical nature of the gospel and the transformational values of the kingdom.

Finally, King's dream of a world transformed by the gospel was a vision for which he was willing to die. When Jesus called people to lay down their lives and take up their cross to follow Him, he was not introducing some shallow pseudo-religious philosophy. He proclaimed the true costs of discipleship to those willing to battle in the war of salvation. King gave himself without reserve to his King—Jesus—and walked the way of the cross for the sake of a lost world.

May we, on this day when we honor the legacy of Dr. Martin Luther King, Jr.—the architect of peaceful change, freedom, compassion and justice—remember the dreams God call us to fulfill.

His words ring out loudly today: "Let us rise up tonight with greater readiness. Let us stand with greater determination. And let us move on in these powerful days, these days of challenge."

PART THREE
Celebration Messages

THE ORIGIN OF THE NATIONAL HOLIDAY

The final passage of the legislation creating the national holiday for Dr. King spanned fifteen years after his tragic death in 1968. The enactment marked the end of a long and sometimes discouraging journey. On reflection, it was much like the path that Dr. King followed to gain preeminence as the nation's and the world's foremost activist for justice and dignity.

The bill wound its way along a labyrinthine course. Never easy. Hopes were raised and then dashed. The movement seemed imperceptible; the obstacles were like mountains. Initially, there were a few sympathizers, followed by thousands, and then there were millions of Americans demanding a holiday in honor of the man who was called the nation's conscience. With the historic action in 1983, Dr. King became only the second American whose birthday has been declared a national holiday.

Follow me as I outline the path of this movement. It began four days after the death of Dr. King and the effort was led by U.S. Rep. John Conyers of Michigan. He introduced a bill that sought to have January 15, Dr. King's birthday, designated as a national holiday.

The bill did not reach the House floor, and it appeared to have died a quiet death. However, the defeat kindled interest in the thought, and Conyers was joined, subsequently, by a relatively small group of people that included family members and some of his closest advisers.

The first few years of the effort were noted more for the failures than for the successes. One writer expressed the views of Reverend Donald McIlvane, a Pittsburgh civil rights activist thusly: "Actually, the pressure for 'Martin Luther King Day' is declining. The first year is was an emotional thing, now it's becoming weaker. Some of the more militant blacks don't appreciate his greatness. Today, the attitude toward Dr. King is one of apathy."

Although a few supporters shared that view, there were some signs of moderate momentum. The supporters began to use the methods that had been successful in the Civil Rights Movement, with the Southern Christian Leadership Conference (SCLC), which Dr. King founded. SCLC started a petition drive in 1969 and Dr. Ralph David Abernathy presented it to President Nixon and Congress.

The petition effort was coupled with the reintroduction of the holiday bill in the House by Rep. Conyers. Sen. Edward Brooke introduced his version of the bill in the Senate. Both bills failed and the petition effort gained few supporters on Capitol Hill or at the White House.

Displaying the movement experience, Abernathy was not deterred. In 1971 he arrived at the nation's Capitol by mule train carrying a second petition with three million signatures. This new petition and the method of its delivery dramatized the degree of grassroots support that now existed.

Rev. Abernathy declared on delivering the petition, "We're going to make this the new national people's day each year, and the people are not going to stand around waiting for Congress to act." Unfortunately the strategy faltered, and its failure made clear that it would require far more than petitions to prod Congress and the White House into designating a national holiday to honor Dr. King.

In spite of that setback, Rep. Conyers and Dr. King's widow realized that locally organized and supported activities would serve a dual purpose. They would stand as a reminder of what Dr. King had fought so hard for, and they would become the foundation for building grassroots support in favor of a national holiday.

Mrs. King said, "We want to bring people out of their separate enclaves for a broad-based coalition. Our major task is to make this holiday a truly American holiday, properly and appropriately observed in every county, city, village and township."

In 1970, Rep. Conyers, joined by 24 other House members, urged 65 mayors to initiate their own proclamations and ceremonies honoring Dr. King. The response was almost immediately embraced. Governor Nelson Rockefeller and Mayor John Lindsay proclaimed January 15 as "Martin Luther King Day."

The governor of Maine followed suit. In 1971 the mayor of St. Louis signed a bill making Dr. King's birthday a city holiday. Over the next three years, three governors and three mayors issued proclamations. Though these statements fell short of an official holiday, they did provide fodder to fuel the fire. Support came forth from the labor movement. In 1970, the 30,000 member National Distributive Workers Union—District 65 in New York City received approval from its leadership to take January 15 off to attend a memorial in honor of Dr. King. Although the time taken off had to be charged against annual leave, thousands attended the rally, and other unions held similar memorials in Los Angeles, Minneapolis, and other cities.

In subsequent years, such rallies and memorials were prevalent around the nation. This recognition signaled organized labor's intent to remain active in the struggle for a national holiday.

In 1975 a serious dent was put into the opposition. The New Jersey State Employees Association and the New Jersey Civil Service Association filed suit, charging that the state legislature's failure to declare January 15 a holiday violated a contractual agreement.

By that time the groups had moved closer to gaining management's recognition of taking January 15 off, in honor of Dr. King, without charging the time off to annual leave. They wanted court approval of their action.

Superior Court Judge Samuel Lennox ruled against the two unions, and the New Jersey appellate court rejected their appeal. The labor groups took their case to the state supreme court, which overturned the previous rulings and granted 61,000 public sector employees a paid holiday in honor of Dr. King.

The ruling provided an important model. It was now possible, on a state level, to obtain court approval to get January 15 as a paid holiday despite the obstacles in state legislatures. The action in New Jersey demonstrated that victories could be won whether or not Congress was ready to declare a national holiday in honor of Dr. King.

During the mid-seventies, New York, Illinois, New Jersey, Connecticut and Massachusetts created legal observances. In 1975 the New York Assembly passed a bill designating the third Sunday in January to honor Dr. King. The "Sunday" bill was signed by Gov. Hugh Carey even though critics pointed out that Sunday was already viewed as an off day.

Illinois was the first state to declare January 15 a statewide holiday. Massachusetts became the second state to legally honor Dr. King with a holiday in 1974.

The Georgia legislature refused, for nine straight years, to pass a state holiday bill. This happened, despite the fact that Dr. King was closely identified with Georgia during his lifetime. Despite the fact that the King Center, which played a lead role in the drive for the holiday, especially through its annual King Week activities, is located in Atlanta. And despite the fact that his portrait hangs in the state capitol.

Nevertheless, holidays and proclamations were sprouting up all over the country like small brush fires. With the election of Jimmy Carter as the 39th president, it was thought that all of the elements were now in place for a renewed interest and commitment for the national holiday.

With the end of the congressional inquiry into Dr. King's assassination in 1979 and the committee's final report came even stronger efforts for passage of a King Holiday bill. President Carter was awarded the Martin Luther King Nonviolent Peace Prize, the King's Center highest award.

President Carter did offer two gestures of support. The first was a commemorative stamp in honor of what would have been Dr. King's 50th birthday. The second was his call for Congress to designate January 15th as a national holiday—a challenge issued at the King Center's birthday observance program in Atlanta.

Now the issue of a national holiday was split on ideological lines. Two months after Sen. Edward Kennedy announced his support during a speech at Atlanta's Ebenezer Baptist Church, he and Sen. Strom Thurmond argued the issue on the Senate floor.

Thurmond questioned whether the nation could afford the national holiday. He estimated that it would cost the federal government $22 million in overtime pay for federal employees alone. Kennedy countered that such an estimate did not consider the revenue that might be generated through the sale of commemorative items sold and tickets purchased for events during a national observance.

Though support was growing, in November 1979, the House rejected Conyer's bill once again. Without House action, the Senate version languished.

Although the bill was defeated, it did gather 133 votes. In 1980 a House motion succeeded in suspending the rules, allowing a two-thirds majority for passage rather than three fourths, which was normally required for national holiday legislation. The rule change meant that now 287 votes would be needed, not 326. The bill fell five shorts of passage.

Despite the defeat, Rep. Conyers remained upbeat. He asserted, "We were short a few votes. But I think the momentum that builds up every year around King is sincere and genuine across America. And I think that we're finally coming to the period where we're going to do it."

By 1981 it was clear that what was needed was to focus the public's heightened awareness. A rallying point was needed to serve as a lightning rod to ignite the brush fires around the country into a firestorm of support for the holiday bill.
That spark came from singer and composer Stevie Wonder's song, "Happy Birthday." That song provided the rod. Like famed entertainers earlier such as Harry Belafonte, Tony Bennett, Roberta Flack, Gil Scot Heron and Diana Ross, Stevie Wonder had long assisted Dr. King and the Civil Rights Movement through his presence, time and money. This time he lent his lawyer and provided her with unlimited financial resources to push the effort.

By the end of 1981 the public was well aware of the song and its purpose, and the ongoing work of long-time holiday backers, and grassroots support intensified. The King Center mounted a petition drive and obtained six million signatures, the largest ever to sign a petition on a single issue.

At the start of the 1982 congressional session the supporters devised a comprehensive lobbying plan and sponsored national legislative strategy sessions. Labor unions, black fraternities and sororities, associations all were mobilized.

State-by-state and district-by-district contact was vigorously pursued by these groups until fall 1982, when Congress reopened after its summer recess. The intensified lobby caused reverberations. Finally there was movement in Congress.

On July 3, 1983, the subcommittee pushing for the holiday passed the bill along to full committee, which approved the legislation and sent it to the House. In August 1983, the House voted 338 to 90 in favor of designating the third Monday in January to honor Dr. King.

Senate opposition to the holiday bill peaked in mid-October, when Sen. Jesse Helms filibustered. He suggested that Dr. King "may have had an explicit but clandestine relationship with the Communist Party" and claimed he needed to see 65,000 pages of FBI files on Dr. King so he could cast "an informed vote." Many saw Helm's assertion and his insistence on seeing the FBI file as a blatant attempt to discredit Dr. King and thereby kill the bill.

His efforts proved fruitless. Although the FBI sent its files, the Senate voted to cut off his filibuster. He then tried, and failed, to get a federal judge to reopen the FBI documents that were sealed in the National Archives until 2027. From the open files, the North Carolina senator presented selected memos and transcripts of FBI wiretaps on Dr. King.

Sen. Daniel Moynihan threw the material on the Senate floor and called it "filth." Sen. Bradley declared that Helms "is playing up to old Jim Crow and all of us know it." In a last-ditch effort, Helms tried to add crippling amendments to the holiday legislation—like having it occur on Sunday and changing the name to National Civil Rights Day.

Those maneuvers also failed and did not dissuade the Senate. On October 19, 1983, with all members present, the Senate voted 78 to 22 in favor of the holiday. On November 3, President Ronald Reagan signed the legislation into law. A long and hard-fought effort that spanned over fifteen years.

I read where Mary Lewis, a Chicago-based freelance writer, said "Dr. King would probably be the first to say that he did not deserve the honor. He would have made us remember those brave men, women, and children who, in the name of justice peacefully faced hostile police with their dogs and clubs. He would have said it was they, not he, who deserved the honor."

But, she continued, "He would have been pleased, because people who shared in his dream stood fast for 15 years to attain their goal. He would have been pleased that their ranks were filled with blacks and whites, with Jews and Christians and with the poor and the rich in lockstep for a common cause. And he would be pleased that through honoring his birthday, the nation will not forget, cannot forget, that all people are equal before the law."

THERE IS NO EASY PATH TO THE DREAM OF UNIVERSAL BROTHERHOOD

"He who passively accepts evil is an much involved in it as he who helps to perpetrate it."

Dr. Martin Luther King, Jr.

Three decades after his death, the Reverend Martin Luther King, Jr.'s words still blaze off the page. His writings on American society remain keen today because his vision extended well beyond the end of segregation. He spoke out for the need for people to reconcile, not just integrate in the workplace and at the lunch counter. And he knew that would take conscious effort, discipline and hope. If America has lagged in achieving his dream, it may be because we did not fully accept that burden of work and hope.

In a 1960 speech to the National Urban League, Dr. King spoke of the changing world economy and warned black Americans to be ready. Now in 1999 his words apply to all Americans:

"We must constantly stimulate our youth to rise above the stagnant level of mediocrity and seek to achieve excellence in their various fields of endeavor . . . We must make it clear to our young people that this is an age in which they will be forced to compete with people of all races

and nationalities . . . We must set out to do a good job irrespective of race. We must seek to do our life's work so well that nobody could do it better."

At the same time, there can be no meritocracy, nor fair competition, if discrimination persists. Dr. King argued that the government must involve itself in correcting the pernicious effects of racism and prejudice.

He articulated the role of government in that National Urban League address. "Government is not the whole answer to the present crisis, but it is important partial answer. Morals cannot be legislated, but behavior can be regulated. The law cannot make an employer love me, but it can prevent him from refusing to hire me because of the color of my skin."

Americans can do more to meet those standards. We can demand more of our children, even those from impoverished homes, and we can demand more of their schools. We can also demand more of the parents to be involved in the education and development of their children. We must ensure that young people have the opportunity to pursue their dreams through education and training.

As Rev. King so eloquently put it, "Through our scientific genius we have made of this world a neighborhood; now through our moral and spiritual development we must make of it a brotherhood. In a real sense, we must all learn to live together as brothers or we will all perish together as fools. We must all live together; we must all be concerned about each other."

RECOGNITION PROGRAM
REMARKS

Anyone who rises to speak on this day, the 20th of January, speaks in the shadow of the glory of some of the most notable phrases ever uttered, phrases spoken by men as they were inaugurated as President of the United States.

Since 1937, January 20th has been designated as Presidential Inauguration Day, when Franklin D. Roosevelt saw "one third of a nation ill-clad, ill-housed, and ill-nourished." When John F. Kennedy urged his fellow Americans to "ask not what your country can do for you, ask what you can do for your country." When Harry S. Truman observed that "the supreme need of our time is for men to learn to live together in peace and harmony." Also the time when Dwight D. Eisenhower said, "whatever America hopes to bring to pass in the world must first come to pass in the heart of America."

Equally notable were the words of Dr. Martin Luther King, Jr. Dr. King, who had that glorious dream of brotherhood and equality, and who did not live to see the progress that has been made up that road.

While progress has been made up that road, were he alive, he would say to us that the task is not over. He would say that we have a moral obligation to continue to examine he human condition, and ask how we can make it better.

He would perhaps also bring to our minds that we, all of us—to some degree—remain like "The Man with the Hoe," whom the poet Edwin Markham has described in a great poem published in 1899:

> *"Bowed by the weight of centuries he leans*
> *Upon his hoe and gazes on the ground;*
> *The emptiness of ages in his face,*
> *And on his back, the burden of the world."*

You are doing something, because you are here participating in this program. I commend and congratulate each of you for taking the high road, for investing your time wisely today in anticipation of realizing significant dividends in the future.

I believe that Dr. King is smiling to see young people preparing themselves for greater service in pursuit of justice and equality when they move into the adult world of service.

In recognition of your active participation in the Martin Luther King, Jr. Leadership Institute, I am pleased to present these certificates to each of you.

EXPOSITORY NOTES OVER THE YEARS

Dr. Martin Luther King, Jr. traveled this nation from coast to coast preaching for freedom and equality for the Black man and for men and women of all races. In his belief that there is good in all men, he sought to elevate man above the evils of prejudice, selfishness and meanness—sins that plague us and prevent us from loving each other as we should.

Because the world realized and understood that Dr. King fought on behalf of all mankind, the whole world mourned his passing. And because of life embraced eternal truths: truth of goodness, of freedom, of compassion for all men, Dr. King left to the world an idea, a faith and a hope that lives on today.

In one of his famous addresses he asked "If we really keep our eyes open and look at the injustices around us, can we not call the time in which we live the world's midnight hour—a time of a beginning and an end, a new day dawning?"

In one of his last public appearances before his tragic and senseless death, the capstone was laid. We remember these words: "I don't know what will happen now. We have got some difficult days ahead, but it doesn't matter with me, because I've been to the mountaintop. Like everyone else, I would like to live a long life.

But I'm not concerned about that. I just want to do God's will, and He has allowed me to go up the mountain."

This excerpt from the famous Memphis address is instructive: "You all know the story of Rip Van Winkle ... Everyone remembers that Winkle slept for twenty years. But what is important is that when he went up on that mountain to sleep there was a picture of King George hanging in the town. When he came down, there was a picture of George Washington in its place."

Dr. King continued . . . "Rip Van Winkle slept through a revolution, but we cannot afford to remain asleep. Our world is a neighborhood. We must all learn to live together as brothers, or we will perish as fools . . ." The record shows that the life of Dr. Martin Luther King, Jr. was one fully committed to education as the foundation for social change and improvement in humankind. And so it with this moment of perspective from his life that we share thoughts with you on this occasion.

MARTIN LUTHER KING, JR.

OBSERVANCE MEDITATION PRAYER

Think on these words of Dr. Martin Luther King, Jr.:

"So I say to you, seek God and discover Him and make Him a power in your life. Without Him, all of our efforts turn to ashes and our sunrises into darkest nights. Without Him, life is a meaningless drama with the decisive scenes missing. But with Him we are able to rise from the fatigue of despair into the buoyancy of hope. With Him we are able to rise from the midnight of desperation to the daybreak of joy.
St. Augustine was right—we were made for God and we will be restless until we find rest in Him.

And so, it is in the spirit of Dr. King that we pray humbly:

Brood over us, O Holy Spirit of God. Infill us with some holy and high purposes for our lives.

Make us available to be instruments through which your light shines into the darkness of the world.

Show us how to be light to those who are lost in the darkness of sin.

Show us how to be light to those who are lost in the depths of suffering.

Show us how to be light to those who are lonely this day, we pray.

Show us how to be light to those with some overshadowing burden.

Show us how to be light to the desperately depressed, we pray.

As we observe this birthday of one of your children, we pray that you will let there be light. Let it comes through to us as we commit ourselves to Him in the example of Dr. Martin Luther King, Jr.

AMEN

THE REAL MEANING OF THE KING HOLIDAY

On January 15th our nation stopped for 24 hours to honor the memory and the life of a Black American—Dr. Martin Luther King, Jr. This national holiday provides an occasion for us to reaffirm our commitment to his dream of freedom for America. We gain strength from his courage on so many battlefields—from the beginning in Montgomery, Alabama in 1955 with the Montgomery Bus Boycott, to the tragic end of his life in Memphis in 1968.

All over America, men, women and little children linked hands and hopes in an unprecedented national holiday for Martin Luther King, Jr. A grandson of a former slave who rose to spiritual heights attained by few mortals and thereby fulfilled the Biblical adage which says that he who is last shall be first.

This astonishing recognition of Black initiative and leadership would have been inconceivable earlier in my lifetime. The national holiday marks a great divide in the relationship between Black and White Americans. For on King Day, Americans of all races, backgrounds and political persuasions, were forced to take official notice not only of Martin Luther King, Jr. but also of the maids, the sharecroppers, the students and the Rosa Parkses who made him what he was.

This is the tradition and the hope that the Martin Luther King, Jr. holiday brings to the nation. And that tradition speaks in and through the King Holiday, telling us that a people who could produce a King have no need for fears or apologies or doubts.

As the first Black American so honored, Martin Luther King, Jr. joined the most exclusive of all American clubs. Ironically, and significantly, the only other American honored by a national holiday is George Washington.

There is irony—and truth—in this. For King and his nonviolent army gave America a new birth of freedom. They banished the Jim Crow signs, browned American politics, and transformed the student movement, the women's movement and the church. And all Americans are indebted to King and the nonviolent liberators who broke into American history like beneficent burglars, bringing with them the gifts of vision, passion and truth. It can be argued that King freed more White people than Black people.

This then, is a national holiday with national implications. And we are called, in and through the holiday, to the national task of continuing the struggle for the fulfillment of King's dream.

The crucial point here and elsewhere is that this is <u>not</u> a holiday for rest and frivolity and play. This is a day for study, struggle and preparation for the victory to come. It is a day set aside for measuring ourselves and America against the terrible yardstick of King's hope. And if we ever loved him, we will use this time to mobilize against the evils he identified in his last article—the evils of racism, militarism, unemployment and violence.

It is on this deep level, and in the context of personal responsibilities, that the King Holiday assumes its true meaning. For it is not enough to celebrate King; it is necessary also to vindicate him by letting his light shine in our own lives.

How Best to Honor Dr. King

We could honor his memory in a thousand ways. I choose to always honor him for the political legacy he gave to the disadvantaged the disenfranchised in America.

His legacy challenges each of us to use the power of politics and public office to pursue equal justice, due process of law, and true liberation of all Americans. It challenges us to believe—as he did—that "injustice anywhere is a threat to justice everywhere" and that "we are caught in an inescapable network of mutuality tied in a single garment of destiny."

What King knew, as did others before him, was that in America political participation is the shortest road to power sharing and to improving the human condition. Law has its limits. Moral suasion has its limits. But politics endures so long as we profess to be a democratic society.

"For years," he said in 1967, "I labored with the idea of reforming the existing institutions of the society, a little change here, and a little change there. Now I feel differently. I think you've got to have a reconstruction of the entire society, a revolution of values."

This non-violent revolution that King envisioned was to rely on direct political action. Clearly, this was the path that King envisioned in his call for a new thrust "powerful enough, dramatic enough, morally appealing enough, so that people of goodwill, the churches, labor, liberals, intellectuals, students, and poor people themselves would begin to put pressure on Congress to achieve the goals of a just society." As one author put it, "racial compassion had to be reinforced by old-fashioned American political quid pro quo."

Dr. Martin Luther King, Jr. gave focus and leadership to the struggle of Black Americans for political empowerment. The cause may have been education, eradication of hunger, jobs, or the right to eat at a restaurant, or take a seat on a bus, but the objective was always the same: to achieve equality and justice; to be heard; to be taken seriously; to be respected; to sit in the legislative and executive chambers; and to take part in the decisions on who gets what, when, and how in our society.

Just before his tragic death, Dr. King saw his dream beginning to become a reality. Street politics moved indoors—into Congress, into state houses, into city halls. And today Black (and Hispanic) elected officials number in the thousands who represent millions of Americans. Their presence assures us that the civil rights movement is far from dead. It is marching to the beat of different drummers. Its leaders are sitting-in at city halls, state legislatures, the Supreme Court, in Cabinet offices, and the United States Congress. They are marching into executive offices. They are challenging the political system with their ideas.

So, once again, we should be thankful for the victories of Dr. King on so many battlefields. Anyone who rises to speak at his national holiday speaks in the shadow of the glory of some of the noblest phrases ever uttered. Since 1937, January 20th has been designated as Presidential Inauguration Day, when Franklin Delano Roosevelt saw "one third of a nation ill-housed, ill-clad, and ill-nourished." When John Fitzgerald Kennedy urged his fellow Americans to "ask not what your country can do for you, ask what you can do for your country?"

When Harry S. Truman observed that "the supreme need of our time is for men to learn to live together in peace and harmony." And when Dwight David Eisenhower said, "whatever America hopes to bring to pass in the world must first come to pass in the heart of America."

Equally noble were the words of Dr. Martin Luther King, Jr., who had that glorious dream of brotherhood and equality, but did not live to see the progress that has been made up that road.

Although not often cited, his Annual Report to the Southern Christian Leadership Conference in 1967 has been viewed as powerful as the "I Have a Dream" speech in 1963. Dr. King wrapped up his annual report address in a similar manner, making bullet points on his vision.

> "Let us be dissatisfied until the tragic walls that separate the outer city of wealth and comfort from the inner city of poverty and despair shall be crushed by the battering rams of the forces of justice."

> "Let us be dissatisfied until those who live on the outskirts of hope are brought into the metropolis of daily security."

> "Let us be dissatisfied until slums are cast into the junk heaps of history and every family will live in a decent, sanitary home."

> "Let us be dissatisfied until the dark yesterdays of segregated schools will be transformed into bright tomorrows of quality integrated education."

> "Let us be dissatisfied until integration is not seen as a problem, but as an opportunity to participate in the beauty of diversity."

> ➤ "Let us dissatisfied until that day when nobody will shout 'White Power!' when nobody will shout, 'Black Power!', but everybody will talk about God's power and human power."

It was Dr. King's legacy that changed the world and us forever. He left us with an immeasurable sense of empowerment with his dream for our communities. He left an unconditional legacy of hope and faith. And from this legacy of hope and faith, Dr. King believed that we would be able to transform the differences and discord within our society into an orchestrated symphony, playing perfectly pitched tunes of freedom, equality, brotherhood and peace.

He never ceased to believe that the Dream and the dreamers would prevail. And if he could speak to us this month from his living grave, he would tell us that nothing can stop us here if we keep the faith of our fathers and mothers, and walk together children and dream together.

It is with this understanding, and this hope, that we honor the memory of an American giant who will be remembered, to appropriate the words of poet Robert E. Hayden, "not with statues' rhetoric, not with legends and poems and wreaths of bronze alone, but with the lives grown out of his life, the lives fleshing his dream of the beautiful, needful thing."

As I close, each year when we celebrate his life and achievements, we are thankful for his victories in pursuit of justice and freedom. We are fired by his inspiration, his example, and his sermons of love and hope. We continue to share his dream that "one day all of the sons of former slaves and sons of former slave owners will be able to sit down together at the table of brotherhood" and that "little black boys and black girls will be able to join hands with their little white boys and white girls as sisters and brothers."

I would appeal to you to heed the call of Dr. King. His words echoed saying: "An individual has not started living until he rises above the narrow confines of his individualistic concerns to the broader concerns of all humanity." He also charged, "All races and nations . . . to be neighborly" and to extend beyond their immediate walls to remove barriers and hurdles and build bridges with seamless boundaries.

While progress has been made, were he alive he would say to us that the task is not over. He would say that we have a moral obligation to continue to examine the human condition and ask how we can make it better.

He would perhaps also bring to our minds that we, all of us to some degree, remain like <u>The Man with the Hoe</u>, whom the poet Edwin Markham described in a great poem published in 1899:

> Bowed by the weight of centuries,
> He leans upon his hoe and gazes on the ground,
> The emptiness of ages in his face,
> And on his back, the burdens of the world.

The burden is there. What are we doing about it? Go in peace my brothers and sisters and keep the dream alive!

This address was delivered at
Cedar Valley College—2007
The Army/Air Force Exchange Service—2008

REMEMBERING

In this annual presentation that I make to the doctoral cohort, I will focus on a recollection of the 40th anniversary of the death of Dr. King, and they will share with you the fifteen-year journey to have a national day to honor him.

While the 40th anniversary of the assassination of the Rev. Dr. Martin Luther King, Jr. evoked deeply troubling memories, it also served as an important milestone in assessing the progress this nation has made and how far we must yet go to transform America.

For many people, the passing of four decades has not diminished the memory of how difficult and uncertain those times were.

There were many dark days, as I tried to reflect in the collection of speeches and articles that were shared with you. In those dark days we wondered, how would the dream survive without Dr. King to lead us toward the Promised Land? You may want to refer to my speech—How Far is the Promised Land?

But history records that sadness and anxiety gave way to determination and action. Dr. King's spirit continued to guide the movement as African Americans began to concentrate on the everyday task of translating hard won rights into representation and influence in our system of governance.

This year, as was true of each year that we observed this national holiday, we honored Dr. King for his bequest of a legacy and a dream that did not die with him, but rather has served as a lodestar for all that has been accomplished since the tragic day of his assassination.

We still recognize that there is much to be done—just as Dr. King did when, in the wake of historic gains in civil and voting rights, he sought to direct our attention to the need for fundamental changes in the political and economic life of the nation, so that justice could truly prevail and opportunity could flow to every American.

On the occasion of celebrating his life and legacy this year, in the talks that I gave, I urged the listeners to commemorate Dr. King's vision and, at the same time, invigorate ourselves with resolve and forbearance to make his dream a reality from sea to shining sea.

Since we observed the national holiday back in January of this year, we have witnessed an unfolding of the dream that Dr. King had with Senator Barak Obama having achieved what many thought was nigh impossible—to become the presumptive candidate for the Democratic presidential nomination, and to have a solid chance to become President!

But today is the day that we call the MLK Day during the Washington Institute. So I want to keep our focus on Dr. King. As I look at your faces and project your ages, it seems to me that an appropriate topic now would be to share with you the origins of just how the MLK national holiday came into being. That difficult process, in my opinion, speaks to the legacy of Dr. King.

How the Quest for a National Holiday Unfolded

THE LEGACY OF DR. KING CALLS FOR MORE STEPS TOWARD HEALING

Each one of us in America has in some way been touched by the dream of Dr. Martin Luther King, Jr. Some of us more directly than others. Some met him or marched with him, or saw him both as a living spokesman representing tremendous audacity and hope for African Americans, as well as a catalyst for change during tumultuous times.

Others who are younger know him because the stories about his life and death have become an integral part of our history. He has become a symbolic giant—a martyr even—in the cause of civil rights.

It is easy to idealize such a national hero, to acclaim his achievements now that he is written into our history books. But it is hard for many to understand what he experienced. How lonely and frustrated and confused and victimized he must have often felt; how frightened he must have been for the safety of his family and others of dark skin; how much effort it must have taken to overcome the hate directed toward him and speak out for Christian values and brotherly love.

Dr. King was a leader not just for African-Americans, but for many whites, and others, who shared his vision of a united world.

I wonder if young persons and those not of that generation can even visualize the racial strife that was rampant in our country during those times. The racial epithets that would be hurled. The terror associated with the sit-in demonstrations and the marches. The jailing and the beatings, and the other attacks on his life. The protest demonstrations. The pain of not being allowed to partake of public accommodations. Everything segregated. Then there were the cattle prods, the attack dogs, the tear gas, the beatings and the lynching.

All of the above represent elements of the struggle that Dr. King was in the forefront for and with.

Dr. King was a tireless proclaimer of the oneness of humankind, and whose most challenging issue in America was to heal its racism. Some in this country still have a hard time accepting the fact that the insidious disease of racism continues to thwart us and poison us.

To become knowledgeable about African American history and to appreciate cultural and racial diversity is perhaps the first step of healing, but there are many more

What would Dr. King want of us today? Certainly not to place him on a pedestal and assume that the struggles are over. He would want to us work on changing our hearts daily and to embrace and support each other. He would want us to continue to work at dialogue, not monologue. He would want to have our young people inherit a better world. A world in which every effort to overcome the barriers of race, gender, religion and background contributes to a vast and universal paradigm shift.

Dr. Wright L. Lassiter Jr.

African Americans cannot do this alone, but we should certainly hold true to his legacy by being in the forefront. We all must participate. As Dr. King said, "let us all hope that the dark clouds of racial prejudice will soon pass away and the deep fog of misunderstanding will be lifted from our fear-drenched communities, and in some not too distant tomorrow the radiant stars of love and brotherhood will shine over our great nation with all their scintillating beauty."

One tradition that has developed around the annual federal holiday is wondering how Dr. King would assess how far we have come. Tallying racial barriers that have been broken since he lived among us is certainly part of that conversation.

For the nation we have witnessed the inauguration of the first black president in this nation. However, keeping track of this type of progress doesn't fully capture the true essence of the holiday, or the man it honors. If King were among us, he would certainly be pleased with the broken barriers and other advances, but it was his nature to inspire grass-roots change.

Indeed, he might be puzzled by how tolerant we have become. As evidenced by the music and movies that stereotype black man and glorify violence and absentee fatherhood. Of black-on-black crime. Of high dropout rates and the rising number of black men incarcerated. Of the continued use of the N-word and racist jokes.

We seem to tolerate much. We tolerate the segregation of our churches. We tolerate low voter turnout among minorities. We tolerate the conventional wisdom that one political party can speak for the diverse set of ideas and aspirations of blacks in America.

In short, we tolerate the belief that there is a white America and a black America, no matter how much we want to join with

President Obama when he speaks of one America (as Dr. King fervently believed).

On this pivotal day of celebration we must continually celebrate the broken barriers. But let us remember that much of the work that remains does not begin or end with the ultimate "first" of a black President of this nation. It begins much closer to home. It begins with each of us.

May it be so and Amen.

GRATITUDE AND THE GIFT OF DR. MARTIN LUTHER KING, JR.

Martin Luther King, Jr. was born and raised in Atlanta, Georgia in the home of a middle-class Black Baptist family. He was formally educated at Morehouse College, Crozier Theological Seminary, and Boston University. The Christian nurturing and personal development he received at home, along with educational training, prepared him to be an outstanding social prophet for the twentieth century. While he is remembered and admired by people around the world for his leadership during the civil rights movement, as an advocate for freedom and justice, his influence in the arena of self-development and economic empowerment was equally important—and significant.

As a social prophet, King was very concerned about the problem of economic exploitation. "He advocated radical economic reform at a societal level and at the level of individual behavior." King believed in Protestant work ethic. He believed that individually we should see our financial responsibility as a sacred responsibility. He also advocated for a society whose economic system would eradicate the dualism of the "have's" and the "have-nots."

Martin Luther King, Jr.'s mission for economic empowerment was grounded in a vision he called the "beloved community." Clearly we cannot forget that at the time of his untimely death he was an advocate for economic empowerment for the garbage workers in Memphis, Tennessee.

King saw both systems of capitalism and communism as being inadequate for producing economic justice. He had lived in a society that practiced capitalism, and he had studied the social philosophy of Karl Marx. King's conclusion was that neither system was sufficient; what we needed was a synthesis of the two. Kenneth L. Smith and Ira G. Zepp, Jr. suggest that, though he never used the term, King's synthesis was a kind of "democratic socialism."

Communism failed to appreciate the value of individual expression and freedom. Communism's emphasis on the collective life created a society of coercing conformity. Capitalism failed to realize that the individual life is interrelated to the collective life.

Capitalism, with its competitive behavior, creates an atmosphere where profit making becomes more important than human need. In his book, <u>Strength to Love</u>, King stated: "We must honestly recognize that truth is not to be found either in traditional capitalism or in Marxism. Each represents a partial truth. Historically, capitalism failed to discern the truth in collective enterprise, and Marxism failed to see the truth in individual enterprise. Nineteenth century capitalism failed to appreciate that life is social and Marxism failed, and still fails, to see that life is individual and social. The Kingdom of God is neither the thesis of individual enterprise nor the antithesis of collective enterprise, but a synthesis which reconciles the truth of both."

The vision of economic empowerment espoused by King was centered on the immediate correction to the problem of Black unemployment, underemployment, and job discrimination. King placed strong emphasis on the role the federal government should play in eradicating the problem of poverty.

We should recall that in 1963 he proposed a "Bill of Rights for the Disadvantaged." He also embraced the 'Freedom Budget for All Americans" developed by the A. Phillip Randolph Institute in 1967. Seven basic economic empowerment objectives were proposed under this plan:

- *To provide full employment for all who are willing and able to work.*
- *To assure decent and adequate wages to all who worked.*
- *To assure a decent living standard.*
- *To wipe out slum ghettos and provide decent homes for all Americans.*
- *To provide decent medical care and adequate educational opportunity.*
- *To purify our air and water and develop our transportation and natural resources on a scale suitable to our growing needs.*
- *To unite sustained full employment with sustained fill production and high economic growth.*

King was committed to a vision of economic empowerment as part of his stand for social justice. His radical economic plans and strategies of nonviolent direct action were designed to raise the consciousness of America about the problem of poverty and the sins of the nation. This was evidenced in the proposed plans that he had for the Poor Peoples Campaign in Washington, D.C>

Although these three Black religious leaders had different approaches in their vision for economic empowerment, the one commonality was that they were working for economic liberation on behalf of the Black community. Malcolm X believed in Black self-development through separation. Rev. Joseph H. Jackson believed in Black self-development through the system of capitalism. Rev. Martin Luther King, Jr. believed in economic justice through transforming government and other social institutions. There is a constructive aspect and interrelatedness with these visions. It is important for us to recognize the value of diversity in unity. A coalition of visions will enable the Black community to better address the multiplicity of issues related to economic justice, and it will enhance the spirit of collective economics.

The problems of economic and social injustice are the products produced by oppression. Mankind has the capability of practicing humanization or dehumanization. Humanization is the act whereby we seek to enhance the lives of others so they can experience with it means to be fully human. Dehumanization is the act whereby we seek to restrict the basic resources of life from others, thus reducing people to objects. The reality of oppression exists because too often people have chosen the practices of dehumanization.

If visions for economic empowerment are to be born and fully realized in the Black community, then there must be what Paulo Freire calls the "pedagogy of the oppressed." This is the process by which we educate people not to accept the conditions prescribed for them by others. Those who act as oppressors and practice economic exploitation want the oppressed to believe that they were created to live in ghettos, they are inherently limited in their intellectual capability, and their limited economic resources is due to their own laziness. When this perception of reality is accepted by the oppressed, they will exercise self-depreciation and oftentimes be fearful of the revolutionary ideas of freedom.

The pedagogy of the oppressed is the process of educating people to see for themselves that the oppressor's prescribed reality is a false reality. Therefore, the purpose of the pedagogy is not to take the oppressor's place, for the oppressor does not represent what it means to be fully human. This educational process is a vital part of any vision for economic empowerment because people in oppressive conditions must have their consciousness raised to fight for justice. It is not enough for leaders to have a consciousness for economic liberation.

Freire states that: "The correct method for revolutionary leadership to employ in the task of liberation is, therefore, not 'libertarian propaganda.' Nor can the leadership merely 'implant' in the oppressed a belief in freedom, thus thinking to win their trust. The correct method lies in dialogue. The conviction of the oppressed that they must fight for their liberation is not a gift bestowed by the revolutionary leadership, but the result of their own conscientizaceo."

As an educational process, the pedagogy of the oppressed is characterized by dialogue. Again, according to Paulo Freire, true dialogue can only exist when the elements of a profound love for the world and man, faith in man's vocation to be more fully human, humility, hope, and the willingness to engage in critical thinking are present.

The Black liberation church is one of the most viable institutions in the Black community for practicing the pedagogy of the oppressed. The themes of liberation and social justice have been and most continue to be a central part of the educational curriculum of the Black church.

It is through education that the captives are set free.

THE CHALLENGE OF HISTORY

We all can be proud of the fact that as we join with others in celebrating the birth and life of Dr. King this year, that this nation can take pride in the fact that his legacy will continue into the future. For we will be celebrating his achievement on an official national holiday very soon. What a fitting tribute that will be.

When I was associated with Morgan State University in Baltimore, it was my pleasure to work with a distinguished historian in the person of Dr. Benjamin Quarles. In his book, The Negro in the Making of America, he makes a pressing case for citizens, and educators, to become even more concerned with history.

He observes, "The role of the Negro in the making of America is, generally speaking, neither well-known, or correctly known." Often, he writes, "the positive contributions of the Negro have escaped the eye of the historian, and hence do not find their way into the pages of the work of the historian. Many books on the American past are silent on the Negro, except for a description of some problem he presented."

In describing the role of other racial groups, writers have tended to stress those traits held by Americans in common. But in treating the Negro, the approach has often been one of "deviation from the norm." Hence, it is not surprising that many readers of history have come to feel that although "the Negro has been among us, he has not been one of us."

Today, we pause to honor a man who was instrumental in transmitting the heritage of people of the black race. A man whose life and commitment brought us through a glorious struggle extending from a darker past into this brighter, but still troubled, present.

As we recount the contributions of our race, it becomes abundantly clear to me that each generation needs greater zeal in conserving and cultivating its past. We are what we remember. If we attempt to blot out our memory of the years of yesterday and its history, we then would lack the motive, the plan, and the power for tomorrow. We become like the amnesia victims in our mental hospitals, who are there because they have lost their memories and their recognition of people and things, as well as their environment.

History can appear to be a dead study with its dead men and women, and its lifeless things. But it can have inspiration and give power in creating a revival of spirit in those who seem to be without life through a living history concept.

This idea appeared to be real in a story in the Old Testament when a band of Moabites traveling along a roadway came upon the open sepulcher of Elisha, the successor to the prophet Elijah, who had died and was placed in it. As the Moabites neared the open sepulcher, carrying the dead body of their comrade, the chronicler of the story writes: "And when the man was let down and touched the bones of Elisha, he revived and stood up."

Here was a man who was dead, and when he passed this sepulcher, he was let down so that he touched the bones of a great man and prophet. Its effect was that he was moved suddenly, stood up on his feet and became a living soul.

However you take this story, a myth or a legend, is unimportant on this occasion. We are seeking a truth from this story. This truth is that contact with the heroic and historic dead Elisha's of the past can have the power to revive us, though also dead, so that we can be made to stand up on our feet and become living and able persons, though once dead in our life's endeavors.

The fact that you are celebrating this event shows that you, and we, know the value of the past, the worth of our history, the merit of Dr. Martin Luther King, Jr.

Nothing inspires people like its history and its great men and women who have blazed he trail ahead of them. Nothing strengthens an institution as it's history. Nothing can affect the lives of black people, and hopefully all citizens, as the proper treatment of the life and contributions of Martin Luther King, Jr.

These words of a young poet at Bishop College, Rayfer Earl'e Mainor have particular relevance as we engage in this activity tonight.

Prologue

To the people that he lead
I have a dream, he said . . .
A dream that every hill will exalt
A dream that violence will halt
A dream that mountains will be made low
A dream that black folk and white folk
Hand in hand will go.

A dream that crooked places will be made straight,
A dream that racial hatred we will eradicate.
The very nature of his soul
To his people he would behold.
Even thought with conception, they would still insist,
Please tell me, what manner of man is this.

This gentle, kind and loving man
Who will be forever known throughout the land?
Who was thrown in jail, often mistreated.
He was always innocent of their cruel deeds,
But he kept on pressing, and continuing his pleads.

With not just let my people go,
But end these wars he hated so.
With not just equality for the black of the land,
But dignity and respect for every man.

He was tired of violence
He was tired of shootings
He was tired of killing
He wanted peace
He wanted love
He wanted freedom fulfilling.

The question came to say, as it left his way,
How much should a human have to pay, before you call him a
man.
The answer bitterly said, not until you're dead.

So Martin found his way to the Promised Land,
Martin kept himself ready, by day and night,
Upholding his battle for freedom his fight.
He would let nothing stand in his way,
No man could make him stop,
Until that blessed day

When he visited the mountaintop,
Then—Then he cried out—world, I'm ready
If this is to pay the price for man
I am not afraid, I'm not worried about it.
For I have seen the Promised Land.

He tried to help somebody
He tried to feed the hungry
He tried to love somebody
He tried to serve humanity.

Now the burden is on you
It really isn't necessarily hard,
But be swift my countrymen, he said, act now,
For mine eyes have seen the glory
Of the coming of the Lord.
O Lord do let thy will be done,
And if in my favor Lord,
Let the hymns of old be sung,
My country 'tis of thee I sing,
O thank God, let freedom ring.
Free at last, free at last.
Thank God almighty, we're free at last.

Although many in this audience know of the Martin Luther King, Jr. chronicle, there is merit in our recounting brief portions of the early experiences of Dr. King after the Montgomery bus boycott episode of his life.

It was in Birmingham that the raw and naked forces of southern law enforcers burst into open and hostile violence against innocent school children, marching and singing with religious fervor about freedom and justice. It was in Birmingham that Martin Luther King, Jr. was arrested, remanded to jail, and condemned by fellow clergymen. They were eight of the top leaders among Protestant, Catholic and Jewish leaders of the city.

They had issued an "Appeal for Law and Order and Common Sense," in which they praised the police and condemned the demonstrators. They did not even accord Dr. King, or his movement, with the dignity of a name. They cautioned "our Negro citizens to withdraw support from demonstrations directed and led by outsiders."

It was in Birmingham that Dr. King went to jail and responded with his famous "Letter from a Birmingham Jail." The letter was widely publicized as a declaration of religious commitment by one of God's prophetic spirits. Like the Apostle Paul, nearly 2,000 years ago in the Macedonian jail, King boldly spoke for truth and right. And his letter became a modern day epistle to those who live by the courage of their convictions. The opening paragraph is meaningful and instructive:

"I think I should give the reason for my being in Birmingham, since you have been influenced by the argument of outsiders coming in. I am here, along with several members of my staff, because we were invited here. I have basic organizational ties here. Just as the eighth century prophets left their little villages and carried their 'thus said the Lord' far beyond the boundaries of their hometown, and just as the Apostle Paul left his little village of Tarsus and carried the gospel of Jesus Christ to practically every hamlet and city of the Greco-Roman world, I too am compelled to carry the gospel of freedom beyond my particular hometown. Like Paul, I must constantly respond to the Macedonian call for aid . . ."

Toward the end of the letter, King reached prophetic heights and waxed eloquent with these timeless words that have universal appeal across the seas and the centuries:

"Oppressed people cannot remain oppressed forever. The urge for freedom will eventually come. This is what happened to the American Negro. Something within has reminded him of his birthright of freedom, something without has reminded him that

he can gain it. Consciously and unconsciously, he has been swept in by what Germans called the 'Zeitgeist,' and with his black brothers of Africa, his brown and yellow brothers of Asia, South America and the Caribbean, he is moving with a sense of cosmic urgency toward the promised land of racial justice."

Then he concluded the letter thusly: "I hope the church as a whole will meet the challenge of this decisive hour. But even if the church does not come to the aid of justice, I have no despair about the future . . . We will win our freedom because the goal of America is freedom . . . we will win our freedom because the sacred heritage of our nation and the eternal will of God are embodied in our aching demands."

That letter of defense soon became a powerful document of faith protesting the evils of bigotry and economic oppression of blacks. It extolled the moral strength of non-violent resistance against unjust laws. It stressed the power of unswerving commitment to the ultimate triumph of truth, justice and love. Its fruits were soon to be dramatically demonstrated when nearly one quarter million men and women from cities across the country marched to Washington on August 23, 1963, for a national declaration of brotherhood, justice and equality for all Americans. They sang, 'we shall not turn back, and we shall overcome.'"

It was then that King, standing at the historic shrine of the Lincoln Memorial, before the statue of the great liberator Abraham Lincoln, that he spoke the words that have etched themselves a lasting niche in the hearts and minds of courageous men and women of faith and freedom everywhere. You remember his opening words—"I have a dream today . . ." I am here to tell you tonight that the dream still lives on!

A few additional comments about the man that we honor on this occasion should be shared. He was a full person. He had wholeness. He was one well-rooted and grounded in eternal purpose and existential realities. This wholeness was largely responsible for his effectiveness. Like a whole bell he sent out sympathetic vibrations and people responded. You should recall the following:

"Tell them on the day of my funeral that I tried to love somebody. Tell them I tried to feed the hungry and lift the fallen. Tell them I tried to be a friend to the friendless.

If I can help somebody as I pass along,
If I can cheer somebody with a gladsome song,
If I can tell somebody that he's traveling wrong,
Then my living shall not be in vain.
If I can live my life as a Christian ought,
If I can convince the world of a truth once wrought,
If I can preach the word as the Master taught,
Then my living shall not have been in vain."

He was a man of the world and wherever he went, he exposed men and institutions of what they were. In time, his life became a thread. His life was a judgment upon the church. It was judgment upon Christianity. It was a judgment upon state and nation. Men knew him as a man who was all that we were and immeasurably more.

So vast and so powerful were the ideals which he embodied that in time he became an institution himself. And this moved men toward the heart of the matter and the jaundiced eyes of the nation. We will not listen to persons, but we are programmed to respond to institutions.

So a Helen Keller is just one woman; but when she reflects the hidden power of the blind and the deaf to master the greatest of physical handicaps, we listen.

Gandhi was just one soft-spoken frail man. But when he became the exponent of the concept of non-violent civil disobedience, we listen. *If it is Ralph Nader citizen—so what? But when it's Ralph Nader, consumer advocate, we respond.*

When it's Jesse Jackson, former associate of Martin Luther King, Jr., and now former head of Operation PUSH in Chicago, we politely nod and say, there are many such. But now that he's the Reverend Jesse Jackson, presidential candidate, we pause and look more closely into the matter he is talking about.

Institutions relate to institutions and Dr. King as an institution became an intolerable threat. A threat because he was the embodiment of the spirit of justice, freedom, and peace.

The life of Martin Luther King, Jr. demonstrated the vulnerability of men and institutions. The institution offers a kind of security and status protection for those who claim membership—so long as they submit to the lifestyle of the institution. This security, however, in time impedes freedom to be, and ultimately endangers the security of the far-sighted.

We are all inmates of one or another kind of institution, and so long as we play the role programmed for us, we have nothing to worry about.

Moses rejected the security of his royal institution, and opted for a risky freedom. Nat Turner heard sounds from another sphere and felt the spiritual empowerment to swap security for freedom, and safety for death. Jesus broke out of the fetters of the Judaic institution and declared his option to be "about his father's business."

King left the quiet, sedate atmosphere of a preacher's study and the pious occupation of comforting a few, to become the voice of prophetic insights that stabbed awake the sleepy nation's conscience.

A man is not really free until he sees something worth dying for. To win victory in the power of love, is to win victory for all men.

Dr. Martin Luther King, Jr.—the whole man whose life like a whole bell still sounds the trumpet of his dream. If his living and dying means anything, let us keep the overtones alive. Let us make them part of us—that we may become the embodiment of ideals that shape the world.

We are descendants and heirs of the legacy of the man. We have the challenge of his heritage which says to us today:

> *Stand erect, and without fear,*
> *And for our foes, let this suffice—*
> *We've bought with our lives.*
> *A rightful son-ship and a daughter-ship here,*
> *And we are ready, as we have been,*
> *To pay the price.*

We have touched the bones of Dr. Martin Luther King, Jr. tonight. Let us stand up on our feet, become living souls and make his work live in our souls. This can be the Challenge of History. The future awaits our answer!

WE TREAD ON THE ROAD MLK PAVED

I spent a couple of hours last week driving and walking along Martin Luther King Jr. Boulevard in Dallas. It seemed like a good place to spend a little time reflecting on one of the most dynamic leaders this country has ever had.

The street itself is rather unspectacular, although it has some notable landmarks: Madison High School, the Dallas Black Chamber of Commerce, Graham's Barbershop, the MLK Community Center and the old Forest Avenue Theater.

There's a string of eateries, from Hardeman's BB-Q to Captain Bill's Seafood and Williams Chicken. There are funeral homes and insurance offices, dry cleaners and beauty salons, liquor stores, a carwash and a church. About two dozen people were hanging around the bus stop in front of the Minyard grocery store at the corner of MLK and Robert B. Cullum Boulevard. As they boarded a DART bus, others trickled in to replace them.

Intersecting Lives

It's a fairly busy street. Still, just about every big city in America, and even some small ones, have a boulevard or a road named after the Rev. Martin Luther King Jr.

Not all of them, however, intersect with a Malcolm X Boulevard. And given how the two men's lives intersected in the '60s, how they followed different paths to reach some common goals, perhaps it's a little ironic that their boulevards could cross each other.

Most of us will spend some time together thinking about Dr. King because he was born January 15, 1929, in Atlanta. On April 4, 1968, he was assassinated by a sniper's bullet on a motel balcony in Memphis, where he had gone to support a strike of poorly paid sanitation workers.

His life was way too short, and I often wonder how much better America might be today if his voice hadn't been so tragically silenced. I said his voice, not his message.

He was such a gifted orator that too often many of us focus on his brilliant capacity to turn heads by turning phrases, and we forget his plea for all of us to uplift humanity by lifting up our brothers and sisters.

He had such a powerful message of peace and hope, and an admirable agenda that called for people, programs and policies to tackle the evils of racism, poverty and war.

While Malcolm urged black people to demand basic human rights "by any means necessary" for most of his life, Dr. King consistently urged nonviolent protests. He stood still in the storm and painted a better picture of what America could become if she treated all her children with kindness, fairness and dignity.

Pioneer of Peace

He won the Nobel Peace Prize in 1964, when he was only 35. His efforts helped spur passage of the Civil Rights Act of 1964 and the Voting Rights Act of 1965. In speech after speech, he stirred the spirits of a people seeking basic civil rights without demonizing those who stood violently in opposition.

Over the years, I've met many people who knew Dr. King and some who marched with him during the turbulent '60s. They marvel at his courage and his passion, his wisdom and determination.

As I drive along MLK Boulevard in Dallas, looking at the people standing on the street named after him, mingling in the community center that also bears his name, I recall where I was the year that Dr. King was assassinated.

I was in kindergarten, sitting in a segregated classroom, two miles away from white kids my own age. It wasn't until three years later that I was able to ride the same buses and share the same teachers.

Dr. King died to make that happen, and that's something to think about the next time you cross his boulevard.

During my years in Dallas I have frequently crossed the paths with one of the outstanding reporters that serve on the Dallas Morning News in the person of James Ragland. This article written by him was published on January 15, 2001.

12th Annual Dr. Martin Luther King, Jr.
Scholarship Breakfast
Omicron Rho Lambda Chapter
Alpha Phi Alpha Fraternity, Inc.
Vicksburg, Mississippi
January 15, 2001

REMEMBER, CELEBRATE, ACT
A DAY ON, NOT A DAY OFF

I will begin my remarks with a story that I trust will capture your attention. A young girl listened intently, eyes glistening brightly as the man inside the television spoke in front of thousands of people about a dream he had for America. Having recently begun to study history, she was intrigued by the black and white pictures in her color television set. She didn't readily recognize the man, but his voice seemed familiar to her, even as a seven-year old child. At the conclusion of his stirring comments, the girl looked at her father and asked who the man on the screen was. "That's Dr. Martin Luther King, Jr.," her father answered proudly, pleased that his child was so in awe of the famous Civil Rights leader.

He explained that the speech seemed familiar because the networks replay the "I Have a Dream" speech every year around the time of his birthday. She continued with the question-and-answer game, wanting to know more about the life of this man she was becoming fascinated with.

And so it is with this moment of perspective from his life, that I will now share some thoughts with you on this occasion of the citywide observance of his life and contributions here in my hometown of Vicksburg, Mississippi.

I want to single out my brother, Rev. Dr. Lewis L. Lassiter, and my brother in Alpha Phi Alpha for his role in causing me to be invited to address you today. Plaudits also to my barber—Eddie Thomas.

The Legacy Left by Dr. King

America has changed much since that day in December 1955 when African-Americans in Alabama formed the Montgomery Improvement Association and elected Martin Luther King, Jr. its president. The demands of the association were modest at first, prepared primarily in response to Rosa Parks arrest for not relinquishing her seat on the bus to a white man.

But the kernel of a dream had been planted and Dr. King's oratory helped provide the incentive to raise it. Listen to these words of him: "If you will protest courageously, and yet with dignity and Christian love, when the history books are written in future generations, the historian will have to pause and say—there lived a great people—a black people—who injected new meaning and dignity into the veins of civilization. This is our challenge and our overwhelming responsibility."

The goals of the African-American leaders grew—from modest ones like bus seating on a first-come, first-served basis, to ones with greater impact like voting rights. Their achievements affected all Americans—with minorities gaining access and power, and ruling whites often chafing at their ill-perceived losses.

As we celebrate his life and legacy in a variety of settings across this nation today, the words of the Civil Rights martyr still resonate in the minds and hearts of many, more than three decades after his untimely sacrificial death.

These words are recited and repeated everywhere: "I have a dream that one day every valley shall be exalted, every hill and mountain shall be made low, and rough places will be made plain, and the crooked places will be made straight, and the glory of the Lord shall be revealed, and all flesh shall see it together."

When Dr. King said those words at the March for Jobs and Justice in Washington, D.C. in 1963, he spoke them into immortality. And while the words live on, some African Americans are concerned that the dream Dr. King envisioned for all people has still not come to fruition for Black Americans nearly four decades later.

The Changes

The revolution in race relations that has occurred and continues in America is noteworthy. First of all for its relative peacefulness, thanks to leaders like Dr. Martin Luther King, Jr., but mainly for the gains the American country has made as a result.

The gains to white American males may be hardest to measure. They gained in moral stature; their souls recognizing the righteousness in making reality out of the phrase "all men are created equal." Materially at the margin, some may have suffered the effects of programs like affirmative action; but society considered the total social gain worth some individual losses for a time.

African-American gains are more visible. The access that was worked for and achieved, in the workplace and the state houses, extended to Hispanics and all minorities as well as women. These groups previously afforded underclass status in American society now are all allowed more opportunity for achievement.

When the Montgomery Improvement Association was created the Congressional Black Caucus was not even a dream. Forty-five years ago, who would have dreamed that a city like Vicksburg, Mississippi would have an African-American mayor, who was elected not once, but twice? Who would have dreamed that across this nation African-Americans hold elected offices at all levels—local, state and national? Who would have dreamed that we had several African-Americans who actually campaigned to become this nation's president? Who would have dreamed that in just a few days this nation will have its first African-American Secretary of State?

Who would have dreamed that a man with Mississippi roots will soon become the U.S. Secretary of Education, and will be charged with the responsibility of carrying out the dream of Dr. King in the arena of education?

All that has transpired since the words of Dr. King were flung into immortality before the Washington Monument in 1963, can be traced back to the actions and influence of him. Were he alive, would he be pleased or proud of what has been accomplished? Let us explore this question.

The Challenge That We Face

In his book, <u>Walking with the Wind</u> (Simon & Schuster—1998), one of the foot soldiers that marched with Dr. King, U.S. Congressman John Lewis said, "There is no denying the distance we have come. But there is a mistaken assumption among many that these signs of progress mean that the battle is over, that the struggle for civil rights is finished, that the problems of segregation were solved in the 60s, and now all we have to deal with are economic issues. That is preposterous."

As he details his involvement in the Civil Rights Movement, Lewis describes his own desire to see African-Americans rise to a greater level and not rest on the laurels achieved in the early years of the Movement.

Peter Johnson, one of the lead organizers in the South during the Civil Rights Movement, and a long-time Dallas resident, agrees with Lewis, calling his sentiments "absolutely right." Johnson has personally witnessed the advances African-Americans have made in America as a result of Dr. King and the other leaders, but also believes there is more to be done.

I agree with both Lewis and Johnson in that we could do more when it comes to encouraging advances in areas like low-income housing, mentoring, educational scholarships, placing a greater emphasis on the importance of education and graduation, and parental support groups. We need the help of strong religious organizations. We need more organizations like this local chapter of Alpha Phi Alpha to take an interest in encouraging young people to prepare themselves to make contributions through their careers and in service to the community.

We need more efficient and effective social services. We still need affordable, high-quality childcare. We lack enough jobs with living wages in minority areas. We still need affordable health care for all citizens.

Although minorities have gained access to education and jobs, they are not always encouraged to seize such opportunities, by being fully prepared. That old dictum that I heard when I was growing up—"you have to be twice as good," still has relevance today. A major hindrance to true equality of opportunity has been the differentiated education and educational expectations that our culture affords minorities and low-income students of all ethnicities.

Peter Johnson often speculates that Dr. King would be disappointed in African-Americans were he to revisit the nation in its current state. "I think Dr. King would have some tough questions for us a nation.

He would want to know why we have a generation of gangsters instead of revolutionaries."

I believe that Dr. King would have the same heartache that I have, when confronted with the fact that African-American males at birth have a 28.5 percent chance of going to prison in their lifetimes and Hispanic males have a 16 percent chance—at birth. While male babies have a 4.4 percent likelihood of incarceration in their lifetimes.

Although historians have placed the term "civil rights" on the legislation that Dr. King was seeking for the underprivileged, I prefer to think of his work as a struggle for moral rights—and that is a struggle that is not over.

Dr. King understood that the issues at hand were not legal but moral. White America was suffering from the disease of racism and to some degree still is. Dr. King was not America's lawyer, but he was a doctor trying to heal the nation's sickness.

Though King gave his life for his people and his nation, the community for which he moved mountains has still not attained the level of liberation they are inherently entitled to

Yes, we have enjoyed the freedoms of the few milestones of the Movement, but I am afraid that we have allowed complacency and self-interest to set in. Many of us have dropped the ball and become too comfortable. We buy into the mentality that victories have been won, when in actuality victories must be viewed as temporary.

I believe that many are still "dreaming" and have not yet awakened to see the current state of affairs as it relates to racism, economic disparity and educational inequities. Dr. King never fought for himself; he fought for the rights of others. I am afraid that many of us have used the legacy of Dr. King as a platform to better ourselves and not our fellowman. Persons who have not been directly affected by racism, or red-lining, or racial profiling, refuse to admit that a problem exists.

The dream of Dr. King was never about "I." We have personalized the dream. We have made it about us and we have forgotten about our other brothers and sisters. That, my friends and brothers, is one of the real tragedies of the dream.

Too many of our brothers and sisters have not been lifted to the mountaintop. They have not been shown the view. Nor have they been taught to make the climb themselves, and that the climb might be worth the effort required.

One of the outspoken African-American leaders in Dallas, County Commissioner John Wiley Price, said he does not believe that Dr. King lived or died in vain. But he is concerned that African Americans are making a mockery of his legacy by sitting around waiting for someone else to do what he charged the community to do. Like Commissioner Price, I sometimes worry that we are always waiting for the next King; the next leader to rise up.

We could be angry with this. We could be sad. But Dr. King called us to a larger challenge and responsibility. One that everyone can embrace. In a televised interview in 1997 on PBS, Bernice King, the youngest of Dr. King's four children, said she was not at all concerned that her father died in vain because his life as part of an "ongoing struggle."

Oh my brothers and sisters, the struggle is indeed continuous and I truly believe that is exactly the way Dr. King intended for it to be. When we listen to the "I Have a Dream" speech at hundreds of community breakfasts, banquets, and forums across this nation today, it is my hope and prayer that the words will live on in the minds of African-Americans and move them to action. I believe that he left some of that speech in all of us . . . so that we would catch fire, and make the dream become a reality.

Let us rise up today with a greater readiness. Let us stand up with a greater determination. And let us move on in these powerful days, these days of challenge, to make America what it ought to be. We have the opportunity to make America a better nation. And I want to thank God once more, for allowing me to be here with you, and to do my part to make the dream a reality.

THE QUEST FOR UNITY AMONG KOREAN AMERICANS AND AFRICAN AMERICANS

To the Honorable General Counsel, Mr. Dae Ha Choi, President Yang S. Kim, President Malcolm Robinson, the honored master of ceremonies, ladies and gentlemen. I am truly honored to have been asked to bring remarks on this the occasion of the third annual Friendship Dinner between our respective chambers of commerce.

These are tenuous times for our nation, your Korean homeland, and for the people here in Dallas, to include Korean and Black business persons. What I shall do is cover two major points in talk. First, I want to share some observations with you about this particular moment in time here in America. Second, I will with you some brief aspects of the work of the President's Commission on Minority Business Development, where I serve as a Commissioner.

A publication came across my desk recently with the heading—"An End to Sanctuary." The text that followed spoke of the end of the current decade—the period of the nineties. Some refer to the last decade of a century as the time-markers of consequence, rather than logic. The calendar dividers separating the end of one century and its epoch from the next. They become moments of reflection as well as anticipation. For American history, we can recite the events of the nineties over time quite easily. Columbus crossed the Atlantic in the 1490s; the 1690s gave us the Salem witchcraft trials; the 1790s saw the forging of the instruments of national power along with the Whiskey Rebellion and the Alien and Sedition Acts; and 1890s turned out to be less than gay, ushering in the worst of all depressions along with the oratory of William Jennings Bryan.

For us who are assembled here, the 1990s are upon us. For the Dallas Korean Chamber of Commerce and the Dallas Black Chamber of Commerce, the decade is likely to prove a troubling end to the century. A time of greater questioning, as well as time of uncertainty. As we assemble here for this third fellowship dinner, we should ask ourselves the question—"How will this century end for us individually and collectively?"

In order for us to answer that question, it would be instructive to look back on the 1980s for a moment. During the 1980s, millions of workers saw jobs disappear, to be replaced, if at all, by jobs paying lower wages or demanding greater education and skills than they possessed.

We discovered in the 1980s that, to succeed in world markets, it was not simply a matter of working harder—we had to work smarter. We discovered that working smarter meant improving the skills and education of our labor force and learning new ways of managing our businesses. We also began to realize that success in the new global marketplace will depend on expanding opportunities and tapping the potential of all of our people.

The new awareness of the essential importance of developing every American's potential has led to a nationwide drive to improve our neglected public schools. We can witness to that with what we see happening here in Dallas.

But as central as education is to a brighter individual and collective future, concentrating on schools alone is not enough. Even the best teachers will be less able to help children who come to school hungry, sleepy, afraid of crime, and expecting to fail.

Rebuilding cities and salvaging people, young and old, from poverty and despair will take efforts that address the whole person, and that offer help ranging from decent health care and decent housing, to job opportunities and safe streets.

We must recommit ourselves to unlocking the talents of those millions of Americans still trapped by poverty and self-doubt. This will take a new commitment by individuals, by the government, by business, and by non-profit organizations—like these two chambers of commerce—all working together toward a common goal.

I believe that this is a crucial moment for America. A time when events have offered us a rare opportunity to reconsider what kind of future we want, not only for ourselves, but also for our children. A time when we can commit to providing the kinds of opportunities that America has been built on. A time when we can pursue that goal with a confidence that has been lacking for too long.

The sense of powerlessness and pessimism that has haunted America since the Vietnam War may finally have been routed. The question we now face is whether we are ready to direct our restored confidence and energies to the problems of our collective future.

The Commission on Minority Business Development

Now let us direct just a few minutes to scratching the surface on at least one initiative of the President's Commission on Minority Business Development. The United States has historically been a model for the world because of our free enterprise system, with its emphasis on entrepreneurship and innovation. Today, however, America has lost ground and momentum in those critical areas. These are some of the reasons. There is no focal point or national policy for entrepreneurship, it is taken for granted; financing and equity capital needed for the growth of small businesses is becoming increasingly difficult to obtain; entrepreneurship without access to capital cannot thrive; growth opportunities resulting in precious jobs are diminishing at an alarming rate, which the economy is further burdened by higher unemployment; a spiraling crime rate and fewer educated citizens; and foreign competition on an exponential growth wave, which makes it more difficult for American businesses to price products and services competitively, both on the domestic and international fronts. Nowhere is this alarming trend more devastating than among America's minority business community, as well as the general populace.

It is forecasted that within twenty to thirty years, our society will have transformed itself into a workforce consisting mostly of women and multiple ethnic groups. Training and in many instances, retraining, is critical to maximize the potential of the growing labor pool. Any segment that is unproductive, unskilled, and uneducated imposes a phenomenal burden on everyone else. Exclusion of a few is a losing proposition and every element and individual within this nation must be brought into play.

A serious deficit of minority entrepreneurs exist which is creating an overall societal problem affecting families, neighborhoods, and the nation as a whole. Lack of businesses headed by minorities located directly within the minority communities is resulting in more unemployment, and increased crime in those immediate areas than elsewhere. All of this contributes to factors which are negatively impacting America's economic condition.

If, on the other hand, we are able to transform an estimated 50 million people (20% of our population), consisting largely of minorities and other disadvantaged persons, into a positive and contributing national resource, we can add hundred of billions of dollars to our Gross National Product. We can also minimize the financial drain of welfare and other subsistence programs by producing viable tax-paying citizens as opposed to people who are dependent upon government programs for survival.

In support of the strength building process, we must create an American theme to minority business development, not a minority slant to American business. This Commission firmly believes that successful minority businesses will never evolve until the public and private sectors stop viewing us as "social causes" and start treating minorities in business as legitimate partners and competitors.

The majority business community still sees minorities in business in a social context, as a part of affirmative action programs and civil rights issues. On the other hand, affirmative action and equal opportunity programs have helped to create decision makers and business leaders among minorities and women throughout all levels of government and the private sector. As a result, a new generation of entrepreneurs from these groups has evolved which has the management experience, the technical skills and other necessary expertise to be successful in business. Fledgling minority entrepreneurs now need access to opportunities. It is the conviction of this Commission that this theme be grounded into the doctrine that what is good for minorities in business is also good for America. Civil rights without economic strength is a borrowed event. It can be taken away at any time.

Congress recognized the need for an independent assessment of all federal government programs that have a leading role in assuring the full participation of small and minority-owned firms in the marketplace. To this end, the Small Business Committee of the House and Senate, led by Congressman John LaFalce and former Senator Lowell Weicker and his successor, Senator Dale Bumpers, created language establishing such an independent assessment body. That body is the U.S. Commission on Minority Business Development. We are recommending that this independent assessment process be ongoing. Further, this body can assist in developing policy, regulations, and legislation to create a broader role for minorities to contribute more fully to the American economic system.

The official activities of the Commission began with the appointment of its chairman in July 1989. The chairman, Joshua Smith, is a successful business owner in Maryland. Following the appointment of the chairman, twelve other individuals from across the nation were selected and sworn into office by the Vice President. I was privileged to be one of the appointees to the Commission.

Since its establishment, the Commission has conducted official hearings across the country; received testimony from over five hundred witnesses; and participated in activities in forty-three states and seventy-one cities; directly interacting with over 100,000 people. Commission representatives have met with members of Congress, Cabinet Secretaries, Federal officials, governors, mayors, city/county officials, as well as entrepreneurs, educators, corporate executives, and small business owners. This involvement has taken commission representatives to college campuses and business and government centers throughout the nation.

As Commissioners, it is our desire that the Congress continue to promote the role of the Federal government in creating a level playing field for all Americans by removing all barriers to economic independence. These barriers include: access to capital, duplicative and cumbersome certification processes, access to new and existing markets, and the negative perception of minority owned businesses. In the Interim Report of the Commission, we have made recommendations addressing each of these barriers. Other areas included in the report are: minority small business and capital ownership development programs; subcontracting; entrepreneurial development; and international trade. Certainly this will require that leadership emanate from the highest levels of government and the private sector, beginning with the President and Congress.

We must all work harder to remove the negative mindset which permeates those who own, serve, and are served by minority-owned businesses. It is time to fully examine the implications of the future composition of America's workforce. And through that examination, realize and leverage the impact that minorities in business can have in preparing and employing that workforce.

It is also time to take a more realistic look at the total contributions of over one million businesses in the United States. Far too often, all minority businesses are thought of in terms of those which are defined by the U.S. Small Business Administration's 3,500 participants in its Section 8(a) program. It is time to fully realize the benefits derived from one of our nation's most underutilized resources in positive and constructive terminology. <u>This Commission has begun to refer to minority-owned businesses as Historically Under-utilized Businesses (HUBs)</u> and to promote its usage nationally. Just as our cover graphic depicts, HUBs are a center of energy for revitalizing our neighborhoods and helping retool our economy.

America clearly needs a return to the themes of entrepreneurship and innovation which made it great. To achieve this, we must have the development and acceptance of new themes and the establishment of new priorities. It is critical for the Administration and Congress to continue to emphasize special growth incentives for small and historically under-utilized businesses. Several proposals have been offered by the Commission that are good for economic expansion and provide for the availability of capital. There needs to be more measurable progress.

It is on that theme that I conclude my talk, and wish us continued success as we seek to build on what I term the "gospel of fellowship among people of goodwill."

A COLLEGE PRESIDENT REMEMBERS JFK

A Presentation In Commemoration of the
30ᵗʰ Anniversary of the Assassination of
John F. Kennedy

November 22, 1993
El Centro College

John F. Kennedy was a man of charm and wit, martyred tragically before he had completed a term as President. Probably his most notable monument for many years was not a collection of papers or a noble building, but rather an idea which survived him and was known throughout the world. It was the Peace Corps born on March 1, 1961. Years later when Jimmy Carter went to the White House, one of the things which commended him to voters was that his mother, when in her sixties, had been a Peace Corps volunteer in India.

The Peace Corps, unlike other American help abroad programs, was not a flow of supplies from a rich nation to poorer ones; it was, literally, a helping hand—it was people who went abroad to share their know-how; to work side-by-side with native farmers and teachers. It is good for us to remember this notable action of President John F. Kennedy. Through the formation of the Peace Corps, as a people we reinforced a notable characteristic of Americans—the giving of themselves.

November 22nd is a date that will always be remembered by everyone who lived through it, as the day in 1963, when a young President was struck down in a brutal assassination. So much of what transpired thereafter was seen on the television screen, causing the event to be vividly engraved on the memories of millions of people around the world.

Questions about the incident have persisted ever since. It is the nature of us humans to ask questions, to wonder, to be skeptical. It was the nature of John F. Kennedy to stand back and look at himself, and sometimes to be amused at what he saw in himself. I would like to think that in this regard he was typical of America. While we are serious in our purposes, we don't always take ourselves too seriously. John F. Kennedy said, in the year he died—". . . if we cannot end now our differences, at least we can make the world safe for diversity." Prophetic words, but not yet realized fully, this quest to make the world safe for diversity.

Chief Justice Earl Warren spoke some wide words at the memorial tribute to President Kennedy two days after the President was killed in 1963. He said, "If we truly love this country, if we truly love justice and mercy, if we fervently want to make this nation better for those who are to follow us, we can at least adjure the hatred that consumes people, the false accusations that divide us, and the bitterness that begets violence."

What Do I Remember?

What do I remember about President Kennedy? I remember a public speaker who had few peers, living or dead. I recall the lyric quality of his speeches, his meticulous attention to audience and *to argument. More than most speakers, Kennedy understood that the purpose of a speech must determine its style. The success of his speeches testifies to that understanding. His June 1963 address to the Irish Parliament will always rank as a true masterpiece. What do I remember about the President? I remember that in the summer of 1963, Kennedy made some of the most memorable speeches of his career. The American University commencement address; the June "report" on Civil Rights; and the speeches at Berlin's Free University and its Rudolph Wilde Platz are among the best pieces of 20ᵗʰ century political oratory in the English language. It is true that those speeches were collaborations between professional speech writers and the President himself. Yet the question isn't who wrote the speeches, but whose vision shaped them, achieving the fine balance between substance and style. It is that balance, that understanding of the language and its uses, which remains fresh and vigorous, a worthy lesson for our own oratory.*

In a recent issue of <u>Newsweek</u> there was a cover story with the title "The Lost World of John Kennedy." The article begins with the statement that—"the country that elected him, watched him govern and mourned his death was a very different America." And so it was. Now, thirty years after his death, John F. Kennedy is fading from focus. Once, all Americans could remember where they were when they heard the awful news on Friday, November 22, 1963. But today the majority of Americans have no memory of 1963, not to mention this date in November of that year. Kennedy remains the nation's most admired president, and the Kennedy family has remained at the center of politics like none other—not the Adams', not the Roosevelt's. Yet, today, Kennedy's magic and the era he inhabited are difficult to recall.

Part of the difference between then and now involves the public's emotional connection to its leaders. In this embittered and cynical time, it is almost impossible to conjure the public infatuation with Kennedy's charm. No other political leader, not even Franklin Roosevelt or Ronald Reagan, has been such a master of rapid repartee and self-deprecating humor. Magic was his self-assurance.

Three decades later, Kennedy's America is distant. And it is "lost" to us in some measure because of the changes that took place as a result of the way he was elected, the way he governed, and the way he died.

Permit me now to take you on a nostalgic personal journey as I share with you my emotions on this day in 1963.

Lassiter's Personal Testimony

Where was I then? I was a young business officer, in my late twenties, at Tuskegee University, the famed historically black college founded by Booker T. Washington, Was it an unusual Friday? No, nothing special. My work involved the supervision of a number of business activities at the college, and I had been engaged in varieties of duties across the 367-acre college campus. I recalled vividly walking into the entrance of my office building—the former office and home of Booker T. Washington called "The Oaks." My office was on the top floor—the third floor. There were no elevators, but it was rather easy for me to bound the three flights of stairs, sometimes as many as 3-4 times a day. In doing so I would pass by the last office occupied by Dr. Washington and gaze at other historical memorabilia.

As I ran up the stairs, I did detect an unusual hushed atmosphere in the building. After all, this was a Friday. Perhaps it was staff anticipation of the upcoming weekend. When I walked into my office my secretary was in tears. I asked, "what has happened? Is there a problem with your daughter, your family?" The whispered response was—"the president has been shot." My quick response was that can't be, I just left the administration building, and even saw President Foster. With tears flowing profusely now, she said, "I mean President Kennedy. He has been shot in Dallas." It was if I had been tackled in a football game and had the wind knocked out of me. My chest was tight. Mouth suddenly dry. Tears beginning to form in my eyes. Speechless.

Carole Simpson, now an ABC national commentator, was the director of public information at Tuskegee. She came over to my office and we just sat quietly, holding hands. Neither of us could talk. How could this be? How could this inspiring, young president be shot by anyone? Who could be so cruel and callous? What was wrong with the people in Dallas? What senseless fools, I said to Carole, could perform such a horrible deed?

You ask, why would I experience such emotions? It is necessary for me to take you back just a little into my personal history for you to understand.

I am old enough to have heard my parents and other relatives talk about the depression. I am old enough to have witnessed the efforts of President Roosevelt to spark the economic revival of this nation following the depression. The WPA, the Civilian Conservation Corps, and all of the other New Deal initiatives that we read of in our history books, I had an opportunity to observe first-hand. I am old enough to have witnessed the entire life of World War II. Old enough to have been born in a state during a time in our history when segregation was the law of the land. A time where there was colored and white water fountains. Colored and white everything. You could go to a department store but you could not try on clothing. There were "back doors," and "upstairs balconies." It was truly a dehumanizing time to be an American.

I am old enough to have witnessed the surprising death, in office, of President Roosevelt and the assumption of the mantle of leadership by a man from a very common background—Harry S. Truman. Old enough to have lived during the time when he brought a human and common touch to the presidency. Not only did President Truman bring a human and common touch, he also began to make strides to break down the walls of segregation. His efforts to break down those walls in the military were just the beginning of social change.

Old enough to have witnessed the change in the guard when a Republican, General Dwight David Eisenhower, was elected to the oval office. Old enough to have observed our entry into the Korean Conflict and to even have served over there myself just a couple of years after the cessation of hostilities.

Old enough to have witnessed the Montgomery Bus Boycott and the early efforts of Martin Luther King, Jr. to strip away the shackles of segregation.

Old enough to have witnessed a young Massachusetts State Senator named John Fitzgerald Kennedy take the audacious early strides toward the presidency. Old enough to have witnessed astounding changes in the political process when he came determined to not only gain the Democratic nomination, but to put a personal brand on the entire process. The debates. The use of television. The return to oratory. The bringing of youth to the political arena for the first time in the then-modern era.

The Early Civil Rights Personal Experience

In late summer 1962, I had completed my graduate studies at Indiana University and had taken my wife and daughter on a motor vacation to be with our friends in Baltimore, Maryland. Just a little earlier that year President Kennedy had signed one of a number of Executive Orders that made it possible for African Americans to have access to public accommodations. We were returning to our home in Tuskegee and it was late at night. We had made it as far as Rome, Georgia and I was just too tired and sleepy to drive any more. So I told my wife that this was a good time to test President Kennedy's executive order. My wife was frightened and afraid that something might happen to us, at night, in this part of Georgia. I was resolute to test the action of President Kennedy. I stopped in front of the Rome Hotel and walked through the front door to the registration desk, not knowing what to expect. But I was armed with the knowledge of what the president had done. To my pleasant surprise when I asked if I could register for the night for my family, I was received with the utmost cordiality. I went back to my car and gathered our luggage; we checked in and went to our room. You never saw so much courtesy.

The next morning my wife (who now had courage) called to the front desk and asked if she could receive an iron and iron board. Within five minutes there was a knock on our door and the request was fulfilled.

We then went downstairs to the restaurant. Again, the utmost cordiality from the waitress. When we sat down at our table, I looked over at the kitchen door and all of the kitchen workers (all African Americans) just came, stared and smiled. The service was impeccable. At some point during our meal one of the workers came by our table and told us how proud they were of us. For you see, we were the first black people to have ever stayed in that hotel in Rome, Georgia.

We continued on our journey back home and I really sang the praises of our president—John Fitzgerald Kennedy.

The Memories of 1963

So much happened in 1963 with OUR president. He brought life to this nation. He instilled hope everywhere he went. We all knew that with his courage, vision, foresight and sensitivity that things would change in our nation—in the world. These quotations from his speeches in 1963, and earlier, typify what I am referring to:

"If a free society cannot help the many who are poor, it cannot save the few who are rich." (Inaugural Address—January 20, 1961)

"We must never forget that art is not a form of propaganda; it a form of truth." (Amherst, Massachusetts—October 26, 1963)

"There are no 'white' or 'colored' signs on the foxholes or graveyards of battle." (June 19, 1963)

"Political activity is the highest responsibility of a citizen." (Democratic nomination speech—October 20, 1960)

"We need men who can dream of things that never were" (Dublin, Ireland—June 28, 1963)

"A child mis-educated is a child lost." (Message to Congress—January 11, 1962)

"All of us do not have equal talent, but all of us should have an equal opportunity to develop our talents." (June 6, 1963)
"Our nation is founded on the principle that observance of the law if the eternal safeguard of liberty and defiance of the law is the surest road to tyranny." (September 20, 1962)

So much happened in 1963; then on that Friday in November we came face to face with a second incidence of an assault on the chief executive of this nation. First there was President Abraham Lincoln, then there was President John Fitzgerald Kennedy. Ironically, both of these legendary and visionary presidents had *been in the forefront of social change in the life of this nation. The lives of both were snuffed out by a bullet.*

During his presidency, John F. Kennedy had to deal with the religion issue, the leadership issue, the bomb issue, the foreign intervention issue, the privacy issue, the civil rights issue, and the use of television to shape public opinion. President Kennedy's civil rights bill was on its way toward passage when he died in Dallas thirty years ago. The country was forever changed with its passage. Reluctantly, only after prodding by others, including his southern vice president, Lyndon B. Johnson, Kennedy helped to end a system of segregation that today few Americans would defend.

John Kennedy's death in November 1963 seemed so dissonant. He died not at the moment of triumph, but in the middle of battle. He seemed not drained of life, but senselessly killed. With his death, we saw many shocking events throughout the 1960s. There were urban riots and campus rebellions, defeats in war, two other assassinations (Robert F. Kennedy and Martin Luther King, Jr.) that made it seem that the old rules no longer applied, and every source of order had literally vanished from the face of the earth.

Kennedy, often incidentally or against his inclinations, transformed the country that elected him. The country had lived with racial segregation and class-warfare politics, in fear of nuclear holocaust and mistrust of differing creeds—but it was also confident of its own goodness and the worthiness of its great institutions. Only in that older America could John F. Kennedy, a Catholic Democrat, preoccupied with foreign policy and willing to make accommodations with segregationists, have changed the nation so thoroughly, for the better while he lived, and for the worse by the way he died.

While the formation of the Peace Corps will stand as a major part of the Kennedy legacy, we should not forget what he did in

October 1963, just one month before his untimely death. Since 1961 he had been caused to lead a crusade initiated by his sister Eunice. Legislation was passed by the Congress that changed forever the treatment of the mentally retarded in this nation. For the most part, this action is nothing more than a mere footnote in the annals of history associated with the Kennedy's. Before the Kennedy administration the mentally ill were warehoused in the most remote sites available.

It all started with an article in the spring 1962 issue of the Saturday Evening Post *written by Eunice Kennedy Shriver, with the blessing of the president and the patriarch of the family—Joseph Kennedy.*

These thoughts represent my remembrances of President John Fitzgerald Kennedy.

Martin Luther King, Jr. Service
First United Methodist Church
Dallas, Texas
January 14, 1997

WHATEVER HAPPENED TO THE DREAM; HOW FAR IS THE PROMISED LAND?

Having had occasion to experience firsthand many aspects of the crusade and battles of Dr. Martin Luther King, Jr., I consider it a rare privilege to be asked to address this assembly in a setting very common to Dr. King—the church.

For today I propose to accomplish these actions in my talk. First, to draw interesting parallels between the lives of two dreamers—Moses and Martin Luther King, Jr. Then I want to take you on a historical journey focusing on the heritage of African Americans who have long held fast to dreams; and to conclude with observations that address the question—what has happened to the dream?, and we will accomplish our final point by addressing the specific questions—How Far Is The Promised Land?

As we begin, I invite your attention to these words of the man that we honor today: "Seek God and discover Him and make Him a power in your life. Without Him all of our efforts turn to ashes and our sunrises into darkest nights. Without Him, life is a meaningless drama, with the decisive scenes missing. But with Him, we are able to rise from the fatigue of despair to the buoyancy of hope."

The Parallel Patterns of Moses and Martin

Jehovah gave Moses an honorable title: Moses, the servant of God. History has accorded King the title of the "Peaceful Warrior."

Moses forsook a princedom in Egypt and chose to suffer affliction with the people of God. King bypassed several college presidencies, remained a resident of the ghetto, and was assassinated while supporting garbage workers in Memphis, Tennessee.

Moses faced his death with courage and confidence. King reported on the evening prior to his death, "I would like to live along life. I'm not fearing any man, but mine eyes have seen the glory of the Lord."

Moses succumbed at a time when Israel was poised for an attack with the land of promises within reach. King was assassinated at a time when he was shifting his tactics with his call for massive civil disobedience campaigns; but his strategic commitment to non-violence remained steadfast.

Moses died in the fullness of strength. King was also in the prime of his life at age thirty-nine.

Moses was carried to the top of Pisgah, also called Mt. Nebo. King proclaimed: "I've been to the mountaintop and I've looked over."

Using these parallels we would assert on this birthday celebration of the life of Dr. Martin Luther King, Jr. that no promise, vision or dream whose source is the Eternal God, ever dissipates because the visionary leader dies.

A Historical Journey

If we fast forward beyond the days of Moses, and his successors Joshua and Caleb, many centuries later there lived a people whose revered homeland was the continent of Africa. Physically linked together in captivity, men, women and children were uprooted from their homeland by colonial slave traders. They were transported by way of the Middle Passage to a place called the New World. The New World was a harrowing nightmare place where millions of slaves died from disease, hunger strikes, and even suicide. According to some of the lower estimates, more than thirteen and a half million slaves were exported to North America, South America, and the West Indies during the slave trading era.

Because slave labor was cheap, the New World became a veritable hell for slaves. It was a kind of Egypt. In an alien land, they felt the searing pain of the master's whip laying bare the tissues of human flesh. They watched friends being mutilated; families divided; others choosing to commit suicide rather than accept the fate consigned to them by their masters.

As slaves worked in the cotton fields of the South, hope was born. As they worked, they composed songs—"sorrow songs"—out of their environment. With eyes of faith, slaves could look beyond their immediate enslavement and translate hope out of their existential situation. As they saw the slave master approaching in a horse-drawn carriage, they sang within their hearts and souls—"one day God is going to send down a chariot for us." So our forefathers sang the words of the ever meaningful—"Swing Low, Sweet Chariot." They pondered the questions raised by Jeremiah earlier—"Is There a Balm in Gilead?" They then would translate the question into a powerful affirmation—"There is a balm in Gilead!"

Before 1800 the dream of freedom became reincarnated in such personalities as Prince Hall, Benjamin Banneker and Richard Allen, and they solidly denounced slavery as inhuman.

In 1800 Gabriel Prosser, Denmark Vesey and Nat Turner rebelled against slavery in a powerful way. In 1827 Samuel Cornish and John Russwurm initiated the first black newspaper called <u>Freedom's Journal</u>, which demanded the end of slavery.

In 1829 Robert Young published his <u>Ethiopian Manifesto</u> that contained a prediction that a black liberator would someday arise and lead his people to freedom. The dream of freedom became reincarnated in David Walker, and he wrote his <u>Appeal</u>, calling upon the slaves to rise up in revolution against their bondage. The dream of freedom invaded Sojourner Truth's mind, and she journeyed throughout the land, crying for justice. Henry Ward Beecher, Henry Highland Garnett, and Frederick Douglas, who so eloquently reminded us that no freedom comes without struggle, also had the dream of freedom. The dream of freedom motivated William Lloyd Garrison, who through his militant journal, <u>The Liberator</u>, became the most outstanding white spokesman for militant abolition.

The dream of freedom became reincarnated in Harriet Tubman who became legitimated as the slaves' hero in her bold stand against slavery as she conducted several hundred persons to freedom by way of the underground railroad. As a slave girl she was called Minti. After she defied the system, they called her Harriet. After she led her people to the promised land of the North, she was revered and called "Black Moses" by her people.

Then the dream toward freedom continued with Lincoln's Emancipation Proclamation and reconstruction in our national history. With forty acres and a mule, some slaves thought the Promised Land had arrived. As a people, African Americans have learned through the midnight of oppression to hold fast to our dreams.

The Prophetic Emergence of King

Then in that long line of visionaries came Martin Luther King, Jr. Born during the beginning of a severe depression, his heart and mind were trained at Morehouse College, Crozier Theological Seminary and Boston University; each of those points and places preparing for the momentous period of the fifties. From Gandhi, King appropriated the method of nonviolent resistance. But from Jesus, he received the motivation of love. From personalism he learned something about the sacredness of human personality, the dignity and worth of the individual before God.

That is why he attached segregation as a monstrous evil that would eventually destroy the segregators as well as the segregated. For the same barriers you erect for others will eventually become prison bars to one's own soul. From the black religious experience he learned that God takes sides with the oppressed and even fights for them.

From Montgomery to Memphis he preached, prayed, planned and strategized. His sermon style and sayings often reflected George F. Hegel's dialectics (thesis—antithesis—synthesis). That is why he was at home as he talked about a transformed nonconformist, or a tough mind and a tender heart. Consider these memorable sermon titles: "Shattered Dreams," "Death of Evil Upon the Seashore," "Love in Action," "Loving Your Enemies," "Pilgrimage to Non-Violence," and "Letter from a Birmingham Jail."

We now must lift up Rosa Parks as the catalyst for the integrationist thrust. December 5, 1955 was destined to be a different day in history. When the bus driver asked Rosa Parks to move to the rear and give up her seat for whites, her refusal was not even an ordinary one. In the words of Dr. King, "she was not planted there by the NAACP, or any other organization, she was planted there by her personal sense of dignity and self-respect." So she was anchored to that seat by the accumulated indignity of days gone by, and the boundless aspirations of generations yet unborn. She was a victim of both the forces of history and the forces of destiny. She had been tracked down by the "spirit of the times." This event set in motion this momentous phase of the black struggle, and King was called in to provide leadership.

Through his leadership the Montgomery Bus Boycott was successful beyond everyone's imagination. After the victory in Montgomery, King went to Atlanta and began his quest for freedom through non-violence. He was there when students marched with Klansmen on one side of the road and students on the other—walking, talking, and protesting in dignity.

In a world that is violence prone, we need to listen once again to the wisdom of this social prophet who lived among us. In one of his first articles he stated that the purpose of the Montgomery boycott was reconciliation, the end was redemption, and the goal was the creation of the beloved community. He further reminded us that "the most creative turn of events in man's long history occurred when man gave up his stone axe and began to cooperate with his neighbor." In order to achieve the beloved community, our loyalties must transcend our race, tribe, class, and our nation. He believed with all his heart that this would lead inevitably to a completed integrated society, a community of love and justice. To King this would be the ideal corporate expression of faith.

King's idealism was kept in check by his realism. He was acutely aware that the kingdom of God is not yet as a universal reality in history; in the present it may exist in such isolated forms as in judgment, in personal devotion, and in group life.

How Far is the Promised Land?

This brings me to the final points in this history lesson for today. Martin is no longer with us. He now belongs to the ages. In April 1968, Martin like Moses, left us on the summit of the mountaintop. Martin left us on the summit of future expectations, on the tableland of a future yet to be, and still in the process of becoming. With strained vision and flowing adrenalin we must ask "How far is the promised land?" When we listen to the commentary of educators and social scientists regarding the number of still-segregated schools in America today, we must ask—how far is the promised land? Follow me as if I offer perspectives.

The promised land is as far away as our refusal to recognize that the choice is no longer that of violence or non-violence. It is, to use the words of Dr. King—"nonviolence or nonexistence."

The promised land is as far away as our unwillingness to work seriously at genuine intergroup and interpersonal living. If we are to reach the promised land, blacks, Hispanics, Asians, and all oppressed peoples must work harder at participation in coalition politics.

The promised land is as far away as our unwillingness to expose and end the sophisticated forms of discrimination against minorities, the subtle forms of institutionalized racism that destroys the social fabric of our society.

The promised land is as far away as this nation's unwillingness to understand what real violence is. Violence occurs when we take wrong approaches to welfare reform. Violence occurs when farmers are paid not to farm, while poor people go undernourished for lack of basic food that sits in storage tanks and bins. Violence occurs when a disproportionate amount of the national budget goes for defense rather than life. Violence occurs when the mass media perpetuates stereotypes under the rubric of objective reporting. So we ask the question again—how far is the promised land? Well, let me tell you something that is.

It is as close as minorities getting themselves together spiritually, educationally, and politically so that we can equally participate in the decision-making areas of this society.

It is as close as our ability to move against the wholesale misuse of dangerous drugs that destroy our best minds before they can fulfill their potential.

It is as close as our faith that truth will ultimately triumph over evil.

It is as close as minorities realizing that we must begin in our own communities to stop killing one another and ripping off one another.

It is our close as our willingness to stop buying the false images of idols and gods of Hollywood and other glitzy cities and create our own role models.

Since the kingdom of this world has not become the kingdoms of our Lord, we must keep the "dream alive," and we must move forward. How far is the promised land? It is up to each of us. A closing word about the man that we honor today.

The Man in Retrospect

Martin Luther King, Jr. was a man of uncompromising faith. This was shown in his radical commitment to pacifism and peaceful protest and in his call for racial and class reconciliation.

He called for justice and righteous living from the people of God. His famous "dream" speech fused the vision of a better world predicted by the gospel, with the contemporary social conditions he sought to change. His faith challenged the separation between the sacred and the secular in the church of his day. He sought to preach and live a holistic gospel that engaged the full needs of humankind with the fullness of the good news of God.

King unrelentingly called for God's people to speak as God would speak, live as God would have them live and to be active instruments of change. Like him, we need to be people of faith. Secure enough in our faith to ask difficult questions and wrestle with the nightmares of our world. We must hold forth the absolutes of truth and love in a society that is so often filled with confusion and bitterness. To live lives of depth and integrity in the face of shallowness and compromise. To light up a beacon of faith in a dark, dark world.

King challenges us to be people of action. Jesus' Great Commission will not be fulfilled by a superficial war of words and theological pronouncements. In modeling the heart of King and proclaiming the truth of Scripture we need to live lives that reflect the radical nature of the gospel and the transformational values of the kingdom.

When Jesus called people to lay down their lives and take up their cross to follow Him, he was not introducing some shallow pseudo-religious philosophy. He proclaimed the true cost of discipleship to those willing to battle in the war of salvation. He gave himself without reserve to his King, God, and walked the way of the cross for the sake of a lost world. May we, on this day when we honor King's legacy of peaceful change, freedom, compassion and justice, remember the dreams of God calls us to fulfill. Remember his words: "Let us rise up tonight with greater readiness. Let us stand with greater determination. And let us move on in these powerful days, these days of challenge."

That is our challenge today, tomorrow and into the future.

PART FOUR
Supporting Messages

By the Author

THE BURDENS OF ISOLATION

Black History Observance
U.S. Department of Commerce
Bureau of the Census Regional Office
Dallas, Texas

Thank you Regional Bell for the kind invitation to join you and your associates as you observe your second annual Black History Week Luncheon. In this experience that we call life, it is useful to have associations and friends. It is encouraging that one can be privileged to have friends who think kindly. In that regard I am grateful that Ms. Beverly Childs thought enough of me to suggest that I should join this organization for this important occasion.

When asked to appear on programs of this nature I make it a practice to share a few moments from Black History at the historical level as a first objective. My second objective is to then move to the current scene with observations of challenge for all of us.

From the time that the black man was brought to this country, against his will, in a state of bondage, he has shown a deep commitment to the successor generation. That is a challenge that individuals in this audience particularly must embrace. I will comment on this later.

I find this poem by Enoc Waters to be so appropriate for a setting like this. Hear his poignant words:

The Only American

The black man is the only American
Who came here not seeking freedom
Because he had been robbed of it;
Not looking for a home
Because he had been snatched from his;
Not as a fugitive from persecution
Because it awaited him;
Not in search of opportunity
Because it was beyond his reach;
Not in pursuit of happiness
Because he had left it behind;
Not hoping for love
Because there was none for him;
And not willingly
Because he came as a slave
In chains . . .

Tremendous progress has been achieved in this nation since the days of slavery. But one area where there has not been enough progress has been the accurate portrayal of what actually took place during that period. Part of the effort to cleanse the United States of racism is to cleanse our educational system of that blight. Certainly, an anti-racist educational system cannot have racist history books; integrated schools require integrated texts.

A basic part of the racist mythology is the denial that the African-derived people have had as significant a history as any other people. Specifically the denial that the American people with an African-derived heritage have had a stirring history of their own and have also played central roles in the entire past of the United States. Accordingly, a basic part of the effort to smash this mythology must be the affirmation and the demonstration of the truth concerning the history of the largest minority group in this nation—the African-derived people.

If this is the goal of the Black History Week/Month activities that are annually scheduled, perhaps the mythology will be smashed.

Now, let us fast forward to the present scene. For this is where the current battle must be fought in the task of widening the circle of opportunity for "all people" in this nation.

Not long before he was gunned down in Memphis, the Rev. Dr. Martin Luther King, Jr. observed that it did no good to be allowed to eat in a restaurant if you had no money to pay for the hamburger. Dr. King, whose birthday was observed last month, made that remark about race and poverty; and it reflected both his achievements and the tragedy of inner city and rural poverty; that neither he nor anyone else has been able to remedy.

When we speak of "keeping the dream alive," we should clearly focus on what was not achieved during the burgeoning civil rights area. There is no serious argument among black scholars and elected officials about the great victory that came from the work of Dr. King. Gaining not only the right to sit at Southern lunch counters, but also access to a fair chance in life marked a revolution in American history. Derrick Bell, a law professor at Harvard, maintains that the Civil Rights Act of 1964, enabling "the children and grandchildren of slaves to make their vision of freedom and independence a reality," reveals the United States as a "chosen nation." William Julius Wilson, a University of Chicago sociologist adds: "The legacy of Dr. King is first of all the expanding black middle class that benefited most from his accomplishments and those of his colleagues."

Dr. Wilson further observes—"I do not think that the accomplishments of Dr. King have benefited significantly the black poor, and he was one of the first black leaders to recognize this," he said. Despite the spectacular victories of the civil rights movement, he recognized, according to Wilson, "that a more fundamental set of problems attacking the black poor had yet to be resolved."

The unfinished business amounts to the undeniable fact that legal equality did not lead to overall equality. In 1968, President Johnson appointed the Kerner Commission to examine the causes of the summer race riots of the year before. The Kerner Report put the blame for the plight of blacks squarely on white racism and its heritage of discrimination, demoralization, and exclusion. The Commission warned that unless major steps were taken, the United States would inevitably become ever more a separate and unequal society.

In many ways, and despite President Lyndon Johnson's Great Society, the worst prognoses of the Kerner Commission may have been too optimistic. In its annual report just issued, the National Urban League again underlines the distress. Startling and disturbing statistics are shared regarding crime, drug use, violent deaths, fatherless homes, teenage pregnancy, infant morality and youth unemployment. They all mark the deterioration of the old ghettos—from which the black middle class has already escaped—and their status as separate and unequal zones of American life.

It is here, in seeking solutions for the remaining tragedy of the underclass that Dr. King's legacy is yet to be realized, and the challenge exists for all of us.

America is a nation where changes in economics and lifestyles occur rapidly and unexpectedly. But it also is a nation where some segments of society are plagued by economic stagnation that continues generation after generation, and seems impervious to government policies. One example of that stagnation is the continuing isolation and poverty of blacks in the old industrial cities and on former plantations in the Deep South.

New light is shed on this condition by the book, <u>Migration and Residential Mobility in the United States</u>, written by Larry Long, a leading demographer for the U.S. Census Bureau, and published recently by the Russell Sage Foundation. Long reports that one of the notable characteristics of Americans—the tendency to pick up and move to another state or region for a better job, or a different style of living—seems to be fading.

The economic discrepancies between regions and states are enormous and fast-changing, more than in earlier post-World War II decades. While Massachusetts, Connecticut, and Arizona are prospering after periods of hard times, Iowa, Louisiana, and Oklahoma are suffering following prosperity in the 1970s. Yet, people in these depressed states seem less inclined than they were in the past to move to places where the jobs are, as workers in Michigan, for example, did in the deep recession of 1982 in migrating to Texas. Our state was then in the bloom of oil production, but now even this state is now a place of high unemployment and huge pockets of human despair.

The impression is that change in the economies of specific regions and states has become so rapid, and their future so uncertain, that many unemployed people in places such as Texas and Idaho would rather "tough it out where they are" than to move.

However, there is another factor. The available jobs in many of the prospering high-tech areas often require more education than many people in depressed states have to offer. This trend of reduced mobility, if continued, could have profound implications for the nation and its policies. The great migrations of the past redistributed the population and changed the face of the country by vastly reducing the differences between regions.

Mobility is difficult for demographers to measure, and some of the statistics are ambiguous because of the way the questions are asked in census surveys. But the statistics, as Long makes clear, do show, without question, a decline in mobility among poor blacks, who in the past "voted with their feet" and moved in massive numbers from the rural South to cities in the North and West. There they remained, still cut off from job opportunities in many cases. Dispirited and distrustful of life in prospering white areas, these poor blacks no longer flee to where they think the jobs might be.

Isolated poor blacks present for leaders of this nation one of the gravest challenges of the century. That being so find a way to assimilate the nation's largest racial minority and end the burden of dependency and the other bitter fruits of poverty.

The burdens of isolation have grown so heavy that, as a nation, we must seize elements of hope for change. All levels of government could at least open housing and job opportunities for low-income families in the growing suburbs and exurbs. Economic development efforts could be extended to depressed rural areas. In the long run, the federal government, if it ever can find new money to spend on domestic programs, could enact targeted revenue-sharing for the government's most depressed by chronically poor minorities.

*As we observe **Black History Month** across our nation, we must collectively seek ways in which our society can shed this painful burden. What is needed most is to find the courage and leadership to do so.*

I am reminded of this comment of a former associate when I served as Morgan State University who spoke to an assembly about his life as a migrant worker. His comments from his own background, seem to be appropriate as we seek to widen the circle of opportunity, through actions and changes in attitude. Dr. Horace Judson states—"Too many see in the migrant only the oppressed, the lost, the hopeless, the uninspired, the violent, the drunk, the insensitive, the short-lived, the uneducated, and the uneducable. They cannot or will not see people who struggle and sacrifice, who love their family, who are sensitive and human beyond all understanding and explanation."

In closing, I offer for your thoughts and reflection: "In the pursuit of happiness half of the world is on the wrong scent. They think it consists in having and getting, and in being served by others. Happiness is really found in giving and serving others!"

I commend you for your concern for the largest racial minority in this nation through this planned activity. God bless you all.

WORKING TOWARD THE DREAM

I want to accomplish two purposes in my talk this morning. First, I want to cause us to recall certain aspects of the life and ministry of Dr. Martin Luther King, Jr. that relate to the annual focus throughout the nation on "the dream." You will observe that my comments will be sermonic in character and form. Second, I will share some observations designed to underscore the challenges that we face, individually and collectively, to continue in the pursuit of the dream as a part of our pilgrimage through the highways and byways of life.

There is a story in the Book of Genesis (37:14-20) that chronicles the experiences of an early dreamer. Joseph, one of the youngest of Jacob's twelve sons, surprised and angered his brothers one day when he told them about two of his dreams.

As would be expected, the elder brothers resented young Joseph for the audacity of his dream, and for his articulation of it to them. Before the brothers could recover from the shock of the first dream, Joseph told them about a second. According to the Scriptures, Joseph's brothers hated him because of his dreams; however his father took note of them.

It was on a hot Wednesday, August 28, 1963, that Martin Luther King, Jr., standing in the twilight of the fading afternoon in the shadow of the Lincoln Memorial in Washington, that he proclaimed for all America, and all of the world to hear his stirring "I Have a Dream" speech. You know the words, or at least some of them, so I won't recite the speech today.

"Well now," Joseph's brothers asked, "what do you do about a little brother who has gotten out of line? We can't discredit him, for that will make father even more protective of him. What do you do about a little brother who dares to make himself our equal or even superior to us?"

On the evening of August 28, 1963, America was also faced with a series of perplexing questions. What do you do about a black man and his dreams? What do you do with a black man who dares to articulate his dreams and aspirations? What do you do to a black man who dreams about equality and a reversal of the whole social and political order? Who talks about exalting valleys, leveling hills, and straightening out the crooked places? What kind of response to you make to him and to his dreams?"

Joseph's brothers said, "Let us attack; let us kill; let us destroy the dreamer. And then, let us tell a lie to cover up what we've done. Let's tell father that a wild beast has devoured him. And after we've disposed of the dreamer, then we shall see what will become of his dreams."

There were those in America whose response to King was to attack. "We will destroy him by discrediting him. We will discredit him first with his family, by spreading all kinds of rumors and gossip about his personal and moral life. We will discredit him with the black community by calling him a thief. There are always those who are open to, ready and willing to receive that kind of gossip. Then we will discredit him with white America by calling him a Communist. Most whites don't understand him and don't know how to cope with him anyway. There are always some who will believe any kind of lie, tale, rumor, or superstition that we circulate about blacks. So let's destroy his credibility first. If that does not work, let us slay the dreamer himself, and cover up what we've done by withholding evidence and telling more lies. Then we shall see what will become of his dreams?"

Perhaps there was one in the group of brothers of Joseph who said, "Well, maybe we're getting too worked up about Joseph and his dream. Just because somebody dreams something doesn't mean it has to come true. After all, dreams can be just fantasy. Let him go ahead and dream. After all, when father dies we will be in charge. We are still the elders, he can't jump over us."

There were those who regarded King's dreams as fantasy. Governor Ross Barnett of Mississippi, Senator Richard Russell of Georgia, Senator Strom Thurmond of South Carolina, Bull Connor, public safety director of Birmingham, Sheriff Jim Clark of Selma, Governor George Wallace of Alabama, J. Edgar Hoover of the F.B.I. They all had been listening. Had King talked to them they would surely have told him that he was fantasizing out of his mind. They probably did say, "The 'nigras' have had their field day in Washington. They've had a good shout and a big picnic. They can go home now believing that they've made some progress, and we can go back to doing business as usual."

However, a few years later when George C. Wallace sat in his wheelchair and crowned the first black queen of the University of Alabama—when just a few years earlier he had stood boldly in the doorway of that same university to block the entrance of the first two black students—it let you know that the dreams of Dr. King were not a fantasy.

A few years later when we observe Strom Thurmond campaigning for black votes in South Carolina, I am reminded that God has a way of leveling hills and exalting valleys.

When we observed Jim Clark in Selma being voted out of office and replaced by a black man, we are reminded that the mighty can be brought down and the lowly exalted. No fantasy my brothers and sisters.

A few years later when this country observed the birthday of Martin Luther King, Jr. and not J. Edgar Hoover or Bull Connors, as a national holiday, I am reminded that God can still make the "first" last the "last" first.

Reuben, Joseph's brother said, "Let's not kill him; let's defer him. Let's sell him into slavery, and file him away in that part of the memory bank labeled deferred and forgotten. And then we will see what becomes of his dreams."

While some attacked the dreamer and his dreams, while some dismissed them as fantasy, others simply filed them away. They simply begged off "the Negro question" and deferred his dream. They put it in the hands of the committee on "benign neglect" and left it there. They told black America, "We are too involved with too many other issues of national importance; we've got a war to fight in Vietnam; we don't have time to be bothered with you."

But what happens to a dream deferred? The great black bard, Langston Hughes once asked: "What happens to a dream deferred?"

> *Does it dry up like a raisin in the sun?*
> *Or fester like a sore—and then run?*
> *Does it stink like rotten meat?*
> *Or crust and sugar over—like a syrupy sweet?*
> *Maybe it just sags like a heavy load.*
> *Or does it explode?*

What does deferment do to the dreamer, and how does it affect the dream? Dreams can turn into nightmares. Everyone knows about King's speech at the March on Washington, but not a whole lot of us have taken the time to read The Trumpet of Conscience, *where King puts on paper his thoughts that his dream was starting to turn into a nightmare. He wrote these words:*

"I must confess to you today that not long after talking about that dream I started seeing it turn into a nightmare . . . I remember the first time that I saw that dream turn into a nightmare, just a few weeks after I had talked about it. It was when four beautiful, unoffending Negro girls were murdered in Birmingham, Alabama. I watched that dream turn into a nightmare as I moved through the ghettoes of the nation and saw my black brothers and sisters perishing on a lonely island of poverty in the midst of a vast ocean of material prosperity, and saw the nation doing nothing to grapple with the Negroes' problem of poverty. I saw that dream turn into a nightmare as I watched my black brothers and sisters in the midst of anger and understandable outrage . . . turns to misguided riots to try to solve that problem."

Did the system finally beat King? Did the attacks kill the dreamer and did the deferment plan kill the dream? The answer to those questions has to be an emphatic and resounding NO!

"Personally the victim of deferred dreams, of blasted hopes; but in spite of that I close today by saying, I still have a dream, because you know you cannot give up on life. If you lose hope, somehow you lose that vitality that keeps life moving, you lose that courage to be, and that quality of life that helps you to go on in spite of it all. And so today, I still have a dream."

That brings us to the second portion of this talk. The question that I pose is—what do you/we, all of us, do to work toward the dream? Where are we vis-à-vis the elusive goal of equality for all?

Had Martin Luther King, Jr. lived, he would undoubtedly look at the world about him today with alarm. Although black Americans have won some considerable gains in the years since his death, the movement he led appears to be in disarray and the gains he can claim considerable credit for achieving, seem in some danger of being destroyed. We are having major inter-group relations problems, and only need to look around us in our city to see evidence of this.

I happen to share the view of some that we can expect a crisis of national proportions unless we move urgently and purposefully to increase our institutional and individual search for common ground; to recognize our common stake; to speak and to listen with respect for our common humanity; and to develop knowledge and thought that will enable us to solve the problems and recognize the importance of our growing diversity.

I was born in Marcus Bottom in the segregated city of Vicksburg, Mississippi. My lot in life growing up was to personally experience raw behavior, insults and acts of indignity. Yet, from my earliest days I was convinced that our nation could rise to meet any difficulty. However, it's most daunting challenge would be its noblest—to reverse the discrimination, inequality, and division among groups in society.

Beginning with the passage of civil rights legislation in 1957, the nation took its first post-Brown step toward ending discrimination. From 1957 until 1980 (a period that spanned the King era), through Republican and Democratic administrations alike, the nation actively pursued remedies that would undo the persistent effects of historical discrimination.

But by the end of the 1970s, efforts to discredit the remedies (does that sound familiar?) because of their supposed limitations, and the discomfort they caused the majority, were beginning to overtake the political and national will. The racial and cultural configurations of the country began to change. To sustain and enjoy the economic euphoria of the 1980s, the growing economic blight of desperate inner cities and rural areas had to be ignored. Riots in a number of urban areas were barely contained; the rate of homicides among young people increased; and incidents of racial and gender harassment and violence became far too frequent occurrences, not only on our college and university campuses, but throughout society.

The language of racial and cultural conciliation was replaced by the language of division, suspicion and fear. Any understanding of the spirit or the effort of the struggle for civil rights—or the conditions that had made it necessary—was lost to the young of the 1980s. Since 1986 on our college campuses incidents of prejudice-based violence have affected between 800,000 and 1 million students annually. The nation's faith in its ability to solve the problems of race and poverty could even be approaching the point of being extinguished. Denial seems to be the order of the day in many circles.

It is encouraging, however, that the organized higher education community appears to be responding to the challenge of diversity with vigor and courage. Being a person of hope, I predict that over the next several years we will see quantifiable results of those efforts in terms of increased minority participation and success. The task that we face, even in the system that I am a part of, is an uneven approach and the fact that many equity issues remain.

Higher education, partnering with organizations like yours, now must lead in developing the body of knowledge, preparing individuals, and building the institutional capacity to deal with the challenge of diversity and inequity, of race and class, not only on our campuses, but in society at large. It is here that we must be like Dr. King. We must move beyond our narrow personal concerns and focus on larger concerns.

Developing the capacity for diversity must become a major focus. This has to begin with the realization that we have no models for creating nationhood from the complex configuration of race and culture that will define our populations in the next several decades. We must accept the fact that no one has all the answers, and that no single remedy responds to the needs of all groups. I dare say that nothing in our professional training equips us to understand and respond competently to the diversity we are facing. Even minorities do not have all the answers.

A second step in developing our capacity for diversity involves envisioning the professional, civic, and social demands of diversity. Blandina Ramirez in a recent article in <u>Educational Record</u> states that the "difficulty we have in achieving a vision of diversity is often reflected in our popular art—what I have come to call the 'Star Trek Syndrome.'"

"The spaceship Enterprise has made its way through several centuries and into the final frontier, and while it readily encounters new civilizations with an array of life forms, its crew does not reflect even today's national demography, much less that of the twenty-fourth century." She continues with that "as long as we maintain a 'Star Trek' vision of our future, we will fail to understand that in developing the capacity for diversity means more than requiring a course on multiculturalism, or adding Alice Walker to the reading list of a literature course. As long as we are unable to envision diversity, we will continue to frame responses to it that are additive, when they need to be transformative.

Leadership at all levels, intent on pursuing equity, diversity, and community in our life is the sine qua non of developing this capacity that I speak of. Especially in the face of economic adversity that affects all sectors of society.

The results of yesterday's Civil Rights Movement have largely accrued to those black Americans who stood poised to enter the doors of opportunity. You, who are seated in front of me at this assembly, have a challenge. Bear in mind that a large portion of our population remains untouched by affirmative action, the civil rights laws of the 60s, or the great debates about goals, targets and quotas today.

This is a struggle too important to be left to the elements of government, the NAACP, and its companion organizations. It is a struggle that all of us must undertake, and there is ample opportunity for us all to serve. The gap is widening between those who have and those who do not. That has hastened the necessity for aggressive political action against those who want to destroy King's dream and replace it with their nightmare.

Holding on to victories won only less than thirty years ago requires that no method or means ought to be discounted. Even one less valued now which appeals to conscience, justice, and fair play ought to be employed. A people at an extremity or disadvantage, cannot afford to turn away from any possible lever that may produce the motive for doing the right thing.

Rodney King put the challenge succinctly following four nights of rage and destruction in Los Angeles: "Please folks—can't we all just get along?" Let me close with these quotations from the dreamer.

"In a multiracial society no group can make it alone. It is a myth to believe that the Irish, the Italians, and the Jews . . . rose to power through separatism. It is true that they stuck together. But their group unity was always enlarged by joining in alliances with other groups such as political machines and trade unions. To succeed in a pluralistic society, and an often hostile one at that, the Negro obviously needs organized strength, but that strength

will only be effective when it is consolidated through constructive alliances with the majority group."

"Our cultural patterns are an amalgam of black and white. Our destiny and futures are tied together. There is no separate black path to power and fulfillment that does not have to interact with white roots. Somewhere along the way the two must join together, black and white together, we shall overcome, and I still believe it."

We must remember the dreamer and his lessons and example. God bless each of you and this organization.

WHITHER AMERICA

Today our world of men does not seem to offer anything that is secure. Nothing seems to be solid. All around us the old foundations are crumbling, falling apart at the seams, from the church house to the White House and Congress.

Our leaders are faltering and decaying, falling by the wayside of greed, hatred, malice, murder, political castration, and general indifference and conformity.

The God of today is money . . . and more money! Power and more power! Prestige and more prestige! The illusive climb up the success hill, often times via another's downfall, has not been what is has been cracked up to be.

One will find that at the top of the success mountain, it is a lonely and empty place . . . a house of illusions, a house of little worth.

Modern America has procured for herself a grand illusion indeed. The illusion being, get yours and get it at any price. It matters not whom you castrate or castigate in the process of your climb up the man's hill. It may cause havoc in the community, the state, the nation, and have repercussions throughout the world . . . but steal all you can in the name of justice and success.

When our elected officials continue to be corrupt with the affairs of our nation and world, we stand at a dangerous place in the annals of mankind. Our history is repeating itself. These happenings are not shocking, nor should not be, to the observer of history and he student of the Holy Bible. For all that is occurring today is predicted in the Word of God.

In the Holy Scriptures we are reminded thusly: "Hast thou not procured this unto thyself, in that thou hast forsaken the Lord thy God, when He led thee by the way" (Jeremiah 2:17). And in Deuteronomy 31:17—"Are not those evils come upon us because our God is not among us?" Today it seems that the god of the average man (black, white, Hispanic, Asian, etc.) is his money, position and power.

Our plight today is our own fault. We would want to lay the blame elsewhere. But it is not the Russians, Iranians, etc. who are at fault—but we, ourselves, the "American Dreamers."

There was a day in which black people had control of their own destinies. Within their families, their limited community (even though they had to live daily lives of meagerness, and endure the brutality and racism of the system) . . . in many ways these black Americans were better off. Having money to spend is not real success.

Drugs, alcohol, mayhem, educational depravity . . . are wiping out our best minds. But you know—we asked for it! We Americans want more. More what? For what? All our modern evils have come upon because God is not among us in our doings. We are too wise in our own "learnedness" to serve God. We think we know it all!

Well, God is omnipresent, He is not among us in that we have not His favor, at this time, in America. Today, the smile of His approval is fast disappearing from our shore. We cannot carry the big stick throughout the world, seeking to police others when corruption, literally pervades and permeates our total society. As some would say, from the church house to the White House!

The sons and daughters of former slaves should never forget how far we have come, or how far God has brought us. It is not necessary for a nation to blaspheme God in order to be lost. All one needs to do is what Americans are now doing. We are going our own way—I believe ways that will lead to destruction and self-alienation.

Every power throughout history, which has turned from God, has found itself a part of yesterday. We Americans may have more churches than any other nation, but we have lost the sense of God in the nation and in our lives.

The most pressing business of the hour is the imperative "to draw near to God that He may draw near to us." Presidents, members of Congress, and leaders will come and go, but the Prince of Peace, our Lord and Savior, the sustainer of divine hope and promise is forever. Unfortunately, His presence with us is often an assumption in our heads instead of an awareness in our hearts. May it not be so with us—this day!

Dr. Martin Luther King, Jr. Observance
Dallas Independent School District
El Centro College
January 1993

EXPOSITORY NOTES AND NOTABLE QUOTATIONS FROM THE LIFE OF DR. MARTIN LUTHER KING, JR.

Dr. Martin Luther King, Jr. traveled this nation from coast to coast preaching for freedom and equality for the black man and for men and women, boys and girls, of all races. In his belief that there is good in all men, he sought to elevate man above the evils of prejudice, selfishness and meanness; sins that plague us and prevent us from loving each other as we should.

Because the world realized and understood that Dr. King fought on behalf of all mankind, the whole world mourned his passing. And because his life embraced eternal truths: truth of goodness, of freedom, of compassion for all men, Dr. King left to the world an idea, a faith and a hope that lives on today. Our gathering here today represents just one aspect of the perpetuation of the legacy of Dr. King.

In one of his famous addresses he asked, "if we really keep our eyes open and look at the injustices around us, can we not call the time in which we live the world's midnight hour—a time of a beginning and an end, a new day dawning?"

In his last public appearance before his tragic and senseless death, the capstone was laid. We remember these words: "I don't know what will happen now. We have got difficult days ahead, but it doesn't matter with me, because I've been to the mountaintop. Like anyone else, I would like to live a long life. But I'm not concerned about that. I just want to do God's will, and He has allowed me to go up the mountain."

Another excerpt from that famous Memphis address was: "You all know the story of Rip Van Winkle . . . Everyone remembers that Winkle slept for twenty years. But what is important is that when he went up on that mountain to sleep there was a picture of King George hanging in the town. When he came down, there was a picture of George Washington it its place."

Dr. King continued . . . "Rip Van Winkle slept through a revolution, but we cannot afford to remain asleep . . . Our world is a neighborhood. We must all learn to live together as brothers or we will all perish as fools."

The record shows that Dr. King's life was fully committed to education as the foundation for social change and improvement in humankind. And so it is with this moment of perspective from his life that we share thoughts with you on this occasion of the citywide observance of his life and contributions here in Dallas.

Other Quotations of Note

➤ *"There are certain things that happen in our lives and in the life of the universe that we can't explain in rational terms. You must live by faith that all suffering has some purpose which the finite man can never comprehend."*

➤ *"You must remember that although Negro colleges are by and large segregated institutions, they're not segregating institutions. If these colleges are properly supported they will survive in an integrated society"*

➤ *"We must learn to live together as brothers or perish together as fools."*

➤ *"The good neighbor looks beyond the external accidents and discerns those inner qualities that make all men human and, therefore, brothers."*

➤ *"The ultimate measure of a man is not where he stands in moments of comfort and convenience, but where he stands at times of challenge and controversy."*

➤ *"In the end, we will remember not the words of our enemies, but the silence of our friends."*

➤ *"I submit that an individual who breaks a law that conscience tells him is unjust, and who willingly accepts the penalty of imprisonment in order to arouse the conscience of the community over its injustice, is in reality expressing the highest respect for the law."*

MAINTAIN THE WORDS AS A LIVING DOCUMENT

In the movie Finding Forrester we learn much about stereotypes and low expectations. An African-American teenager from the South Bronx has used his athletic talents as a star basketball player to win a scholarship to a prestigious private school.

But when Jamal Wallace shows equally strong writing skills in his English class, his teacher assumes his work has been plagiarized. Professor Crawford concludes that a young man from a black ghetto can certainly be a good athlete, but not a good writer.

The reclusive novelist William Forrester, who has taken Jamal under his wing when he recognizes the skills that others refuse to see, encourages the teenager to challenge his professor's racist assumptions.

He sums up the price of low expectations. "If we wait too long, we risk learning that life is not a game that is won or lost. It is a game that, too often, simply isn't played."

How often did Martin Luther King, Jr. deliver that same message when he waged his tireless and sometimes lonely battle for racial equality?

He urged African-Americans not to let themselves be defined by others. In his "I Have a Dream" speech, Dr. King expressed hope that his four children "will one day live in a nation where they will be judged not by the color of their skin but by the content of their character."

Today, 72 years after Dr. King's birth, that dream still remains elusive for millions of people of color in America.

Doors that were closed during Dr. King's struggles with our segregated society in the 1960's have been opened. Job opportunities that were off limits to African-Americans and Hispanics during the civil rights movement are now available to all races.

Dallas certainly reflects the transformation through those who hold the highest public offices. The mayor and police chief are African-American. And so is the chairman of the Greater

Dallas Chamber of Commerce board. The city manager is Hispanic. The chairman of the board of the United Way of Dallas is African-American (for the first time). And for the first time in Dallas history, most of the members of the City Council are minorities.

But the quest that eventually cost Martin Luther King, Jr. his life is far from over. Nearly 33 years after the assassin gunned down Dr. King in Memphis, the percentage of African-American families still living in poverty is disappointingly high. And so is the school dropout rate for young blacks and Hispanics.

With the surging growth of the Hispanic population in Texas, California, Florida and elsewhere, a new set of societal challenges has emerged that were not so apparent during Dr. King's days.

The problems are different and far more complex. But the words spoken by Dr. King remain just as valid.

Writing in 1963 about public resistance to the changes that equal rights would bring, he said, "The ultimate measure of a man is not where he stands in moments of comfort and convenience, but where he stands at times of challenge and controversy."

As we honor Dr. King on his birthday, it is important for Americans to maintain his words as a living document rather than a written chapter in this nation's history.

On the night before he was slain, Martin Luther King, Jr. seemed to sense his time was nearing an end. "I just want to do God's will," he told a gathering of supporters. "And he's allowed me to go up to the mountain. And I've looked over, and I've seen the Promised Land. I may not get there with you, but I want you to know tonight that we as a people will get to the Promised Land. So, I'm happy tonight. I'm not worried about anything. I'm not *fearing any man. Mine eyes have seen the glory of the coming of the Lord."*

The Promised Land is indeed within reach. And through his message that has touched the world for more than four decades, Dr. King is still on the mountain showing the way.

An editorial on the Martin Luther King, Jr. Day celebration in the <u>Dallas Morning News</u>—January 2007, reprinted with permission.

PROGRESS, YET FRACTURED

No one ever completely escapes the past, nor should they. History provides texture, context and motivation to generational struggles that paradoxically are both unique and universal. The African-American experience is personal and yet communal, something Martin Luther King Jr. so richly understood.

King, whose birthday we celebrate today, saw the struggle from slavery to freedom as a passage from bondage to the Promised Land. Slavery wasn't an excuse for the disadvantages that generations of African-Americans faced. Instead, the existence of slavery and, later, of hostile Jim Crow laws were the reasons King persevered.

Virtually no one would questions that African-Americans today are far better off than in the overtly racist climates of earlier decades, when opportunities and hopes were violently quashed. Today's "black America" bears no resemblance to that term's meaning when the evils of segregation set its boundaries. And a time will soon come—if it hasn't arrived—when most African-Americans will have had no direct experience with Jim Crow racism and is poisons. Yet, progress remains relative and quite uneven.

"Black America" today consists of more separate stories than communal experiences, a defining theme that Washington

Post columnist Eugene Robinson explores in his new book, <u>Disintegration: The Splintering of Black America</u>. This, notes Robinson, is the ironic conflict between "the absolute belief in Dr. King's dream that all be judged by the content of their character, (and) the other, a fierce determination that African-American history and culture be not only revered but also perpetuated."

Often, this conflict has represented a Pyrrhic tradeoff in the years since King's assassination—incomplete progress and new struggles over racial identity, expectations, solutions and even language. "Increasingly between the abandoned and the rest of black America," writes Robinson, "there is failure to communicate, much less comprehend." And as such, he continues, "it is inconceivable that the president of the United States could see himself, or have others see him as a 'black leader.'"

On this day set aside to honor the civil rights leader, one can't help but wonder how Dr. King would have addressed the complex reality of a much larger mainstream middle class, a disturbingly large abandoned and dysfunctional underclass, a powerful and wealthy black elite, and those of mixed race, who like the president himself, are becoming a larger, more visible part of American culture.

Remembering the past, and collectively transcending it as our nation grapples with its challenges, is perhaps the most appropriate way to pay tribute to the righteous trek that King pursued with unparalleled energy, and purpose.

An editorial on the Martin Luther King Jr. Day celebration in the <u>Dallas Morning News</u>—January 17, 2011, reprinted with permission.

REMEMBERING WITH VISIONS FOR THE FUTURE

My brief talk with you today will focus on symbols and Dr. Martin Luther King, Jr. America is the symbol of the free world—indeed, even its firstborn and heir. However, America is also the symbol of something else more profound and more meaningful. America is the only nation on earth called a "dream." The "American Dream" could be reality, and millions of immigrants to this land have come here with that hope. Unfortunately, America can also be a nightmare should it ever forget the dream highlighted by a certain American.

Enter Dr. Martin Luther King, Jr. who was not just a warrior for the equality of all people, and the rule of international morality. He was a master of symbols and signs. He was a learned man, a visionary, and a prophet of our days who died drying to save the American dream by reminding us of it. He knew that without change, the dream, and the American way of life, would die on its own.

There were people in the U.S. that were dying; not only of lynching and poor living conditions, but of mental cruelty and fear. King came out of this dynamic setting and challenged the American system to change. Soon, non-violent protest became a major vehicle for the needed changes. Marches and sit-in's must have numbered in the hundreds. People were beaten, bombed, murdered, and imprisoned in response. These actions and practices were engaged in as appeals to morality had failed.

What was it that ultimately gained the nation's attention? What finally fueled the forces of change in our country? What event is King most remembered for? Without question is has to be that which propelled him into the consciousness of us all—the bus boycott in Montgomery, Alabama. A southern bus company lost a lot of money in that process. Someone spoke, and someone listened. The machinery of change began to move.

What King revealed through that signature action should have chilled our souls. The nation should have been shamed. King was praised for his ingenuity and savvy. He was also damned and brutally criticized. Yet, he showed that if morality would not move our country to action, surely money, or the loss of it, would.

Several years later in Washington, D.C., Dr. King stood before the Lincoln Memorial, a monument that was a symbol of emancipation. He stood, looking down into the Reflecting Pool (a symbol of introspection), looking across the Mall to the Washington Monument (a symbol of our nation's founder and the ideals upon which this nation was founded). In so many eloquent words, King told the nation it must choose. Would it be moved by the appetites of its coffers or its ideals? Would people be forgotten and ignored in the midst of a free market system that surged ahead with so much success and promise?

Before the more than 200,000 people who had gathered could respond, he said—"I have a dream . . ."

The Rev. Dr. Martin Luther King, Jr. had hoped to be an inspiring preacher in a quiet, small community. Instead he was propelled by a dream. And by the time of his untimely and cruel death at the tender adult age of 39, he had done much to actualize the dream.

> ➤ *Received the Nobel Peace Prize;*
> ➤ *Been considered the chief exponent of non-violence;*
> ➤ *Been considered a symbol of courage and hope for oppressed people everywhere;*
> ➤ *Organized the remarkable Southern Christian Leadership Conference;*
> ➤ *Had a clear understanding of Jesus Christ;*
> ➤ *Perceived, realized and manifested the true and real presence and power of the human will;*
> ➤ *Brought about a togetherness between blacks and whites never before even dreamed;*
> ➤ *Encouraged in the masses of blacks sublime courage, a willingness to suffer for what is right, and an amazing discipline in the midst of great provocation; and*
> ➤ *Led tens of millions of people into shattering the system of Southern segregation; splintering it beyond any possibility of restoration.*

The Expressions of Dr. King

More than anything else, Dr. King brought a new and higher dimension of human dignity to the Black experience. King was a loving man who was completely devoted to nonviolence with a belief that America could be transformed into a society of love, justice, peace, and brotherhood in which all men could really be brothers.

As we assemble here today to celebrate his life, and his many contributions to humankind, be reminded of two excerpts from talks of Dr. King that can stand us in good stead as we "remember, with visions for the future."

The first relates to service. King said: "Everybody can be great for everyone can serve. You don't have to have a college degree to serve. You don't have to make your subject and verb agree to serve. You don't have to know about Plato and Aristotle to serve. You don't have to know Einstein's theory of relativity to serve. You don't have to know the second theory of thermodynamics in physics to serve. You only need a heart full of grace. A soul generated by love."

"There is so much frustration in the world because we have relied on gods rather than God. We have genuflected before the god of science only to find that it has given us the atomic bomb, producing fears and anxieties that science can never mitigate. We have worshipped the god of pleasure only to discover that thrills play out and sensations are short-lived. We have bowed before the god of money only to learn that there are such things as love and friendship that money cannot buy, and that in a world of possible depressions, stock market crashes, and bad business investments, money is a rather uncertain deity. These transitory gods are not able to bring happiness to the human heart. Only God is able. It is faith in Him that we must rediscover."

King then went on to say in another speech as I conclude these powerful words: "So, I say to you, seek God and discover Him and make Him a power in your life. Without Him all of our efforts turn to ashes and our sunrises turn into darkest nights. Without Him, life is a meaningless drama with the decisive scenes missing. But with Him, we are able to rise from the fatigue of despair to the buoyancy of hope. With Him, we are able to rise from the midnight of desperation to the daybreak of joy. St. Augustine was right—we were made for God and we will be restless until we find rest in Him."

"Love yourself, if that means rational, healthy, and moral self-interest. You are commanded to do that. That is the length of life. Love your neighbor as you love yourself. You are commanded

to do that. That is the breath of life. But never forget that there is a first and even greater commandment—'Love the Lord thy God with all thine heart and all thy soul and all thy mind.' This is the height of life. And when you do this you live the complete life."

The dream of Dr. King is still evolving and being realized. It's full realization and manifestation will depend on you and me. May God bless each of us.

SOMETHING TO LIVE BY

As Dallas Baptist University observes and celebrates the 1990 observance of Black History Month, it occurs to me that there may be merit in sharing an opening thought regarding the work of the steward and the plan of God. I will use biblical examples to express this thought.

As I look through the record of biblical history and human social history, I see acted out on the stage of life the constant struggle between the idea of the steward and the plan of God. For example, Abraham had an idea resulting from the failure of his faith to nurture his hope, and his hope failed to give patience to his faith. His idea was to have a son, but his way. For him, God was not acting fast enough. So, in keeping with the law of that time and place, he convinced his wife Sarah to allow him to have a child with their servant. But God had a plan that was different from Abraham's and we know the rest of that story—as Paul Harvey would say.

Paul had an idea. Paul's idea was to denounce the church, to destroy the church, to hate the church. But God had a plan. Because of God's plan, Paul became one of the greatest stewards to proclaim the faith. The one who set out to destroy the church became its greatest builder.

Almost from the time that this country was founded, there were those who had the idea that slaves represented a valuable commodity. The same was true of indentured servants. There was the idea that we could build a prosperous nation on the backs of other humans that were considered somehow subhuman. But God had a plan.

In the 1960s a governor of Alabama had an idea. It was his intention to program a Black person out of everything which was necessary and beneficial. But God had a plan.

Rosa Parks had an idea. She wanted to rest her tired feet after a long day at work. God had a plan for Rosa Parks and we also know the rest of that story.

Martin Luther King, Jr. had an idea that he would pursue a quality education and lead a life as a minister with an historic Black church—a prominent historical church. But God had a greater plan for his life.

Carter G. Woodson who founded the Association for the Study of Negro Life and History had an idea. His idea was that he would devote his life to teaching and education, in the traditional manner. But God had a greater plan for his life. The greater plan for his life caused him to leave the teaching field, with dismay and disgust, and dedicate his life to the unrewarding and unappreciated task of being a missionary for the truth. A person who would devote his very being to the task of causing the history books of this nation to accurately reflect the contributions of all of its citizens.

Although he left the traditional teaching arena, he was an educator beyond peer in a different respect. He became the first distinguished African-American history specialist. To his credit that which began as Negro History Week in 1926, with the passage of time, became Black History Month in 1975. Of the *sixteen books that he authored, the <u>Mis-Education of the Negro</u> still ranks in the upper strata of books without parallel.*

Dr. Woodson, who lived from 1875 to 1950, participated for over forty years in the education of all races of people, all over the world, in all grades from elementary to college. He strongly believed that every individual should be given unlimited opportunity to make the most of themselves. One aspect needed in order for we, as human—irrespective of race, to achieve our success is careful study of ourselves and what our environment requires of us. This knowledge is obtained by studying, understanding, and knowing about our history and culture. This distinguished historian had an idea, but God had a greater plan for him and his work—the results of which are being lived out in our lives today.

Turing our gaze once again on the world landscape, I contend that we are witnessing examples of steward's ideas being incongruent with God's plans. You see, when the steward's idea and God's plan conflict, it is no time to take a bad idea and join it with other bad ideas, making it twice the child of the devil.

It is time for the steward to repent of the ideas which dishonor, which dehumanize, which demean, which degrade. It is time to repent of the purposes which betray. It is time to change his/her attitude toward self, toward neighbor, toward God, and discover that the kingdom of God is at hand to experience.

It is time to repent, to change one's mind, so that one can experience the realm of God "where unity overcomes estrangement, where forgiveness heals guilt, and where joy conquers despair."

When the idea of the steward conflicts with the plan of God, it is time for the steward to remember the words of 11 Peter 1:5-7: "To faith add virtue, and to virtue, knowledge, and to knowledge self-control, and to self-control steadfastness, and to steadfastness godliness, and to godliness brotherly affection, and to brotherly affection, love.

Although not a theologian, that was also the message of Carter G. Woodson as he labored and traveled on a lonely journey. If there is a message that we can learn from he who planted the seed for that which we observe now, it is a message of steadfastness.

The Greeks had a legend about a fellow named Sisphuus who was condemned to rolling a large boulder up a hill, and each time he reached the top it would roll down to he the bottom again. Sisyphus was condemned for eternity to that frustrating task. The legend has lived, no doubt, because we all seem to be the progeny of Sisyphus, patiently pushing our boulders uphill.

The Bible has a good word for those who have that spirit of diligence. They are what we call as being "steadfast." Being steadfast isn't too exciting. It's probably the dullest of all the virtues. Even the word steadfast has a heavy, stolid, lifeless sound to it. There aren't many thrills in being steadfast.

Yet the Bible has great commendation for those who have this quality. As a vital virtue, however unglamorous, it may appear. Great are the rewards of those who champion steadfastness. That is why Hosea urges his people to "press on" and then cites the familiar statement that God desires "steadfast love and not sacrifice" (Hosea 6:1-6), a verse restated by Jesus in Matthew 9:9-13. In Romans, Abraham is used as a model of steadfastness. In Romans 4:20 we read "No distrust made him waver." Each of those passages is a call to steady, unwavering loyalty.

Steadfastness matures slowly, but like a long-term savings certificate, it will bring its ultimate pay-off. We all need steadfastness. The person who is not anchored in God has no power to resist the physical and moral blandishments of the world.

A great violinist Sarasate was once called a genius by a famous critic. "Genius!" he snorted. "I practiced 14 hours a day for 37 years, and now they call me a genius." Greatness is the child of diligent and persevering steadfastness, so why give up? Why not persevere!

Carter Woodson, and many other notable pioneers had not only steadfastness, but they had faith. They had faith to go on when all of life's circumstances were against them. He was discredited in his maturing years. Persons who had been ardent supporters of him earlier became his strongest and most strident opponents. They even went to great lengths to ensure that he would not receive funding to support his writing, and the Association for the Study of Negro Life and History. But he never gave up. He fought on until he died. He had faith. And perhaps there is a final message there for all of us.

There is always a struggle between faith and doubt. Faith always speaks of inspiration and encouragement. Doubt always speaks of discouragement and despair. Faith tells us that all things are possible; while doubt says we can accomplish nothing.

Faith says that through our belief in God, and our efforts, victory will be ours. Doubt says that you are defeated before you even start.

Doubt has never achieved anything. It has never planted a tree; never written a book; never comforted the weary; never healed the sick; never rewarded a child; never solved a problem; never won a case; never made a team; and never enjoyed a victory.

But by faith we are able to accomplish all that we do. It is by faith that the surgeon picks up his scalpel; by faith the engineer builds a bridge; by faith the pilot flies his aircraft; by faith that the unskilled receives training; by faith that the unemployed find jobs; and by faith that men of goodwill, and all races, work together.

It is by faith that when African-American children begin each day of the school year uttering these powerful words: "I pledge allegiance to the flag of the United States of America and to the Republic for which it stands; one nation under God, indivisible, with liberty and justice for all," they know full well that liberty and justice for all its citizens is not yet a reality. But they utter the words and hold on, as their forebears did, through faith.

Our slave forebears said it well: "I will wait on the Lord; I will wait on the Lord; I will wait on the Lord—till I die." Let's pursue faith a little deeper.

It is by faith that Booker T. Washington created the famed Tuskegee Institute. It is by faith that W.E.B. duBois founded the NAACP. It is by faith that Jesse Owens lectured to Hitler with his feet. It is by faith that Justice Thurgood Marshall sits on the U.S. Supreme Court today. It is by faith that Dr. Charles Drew discovered blood plasma. It is by faith that George Washington Carver took the lowly peanut and invented hundreds of uses for it. It is by faith that Vernon Jordan fought the battle and kept the National Urban League together during turbulent times. It is by faith that Joseph Lowery holds the Southern Christian Leadership Conference when many say that the civil rights movement is over.

It is by faith that the Bill Cosby Show depicts a positive image of African-American people and enjoys a continual good rating. It is by faith that John Johnson, publisher of <u>Ebony</u> and <u>Jet</u> made the commitment that "I will bring to America the victories, struggles, and heartaches of black people not told by anyone else."

In spite of these examples, and many more that could be cited, the struggle must continue, so that by faith we can all do great things. Just as our forebears and the pioneers never gave up, we too must not give up. We must be ever united to work to create a world of brotherly love, unity, and peace. We can acknowledge that we have come this far by faith. This assembly can also acknowledge that it will by faith that we will be free and we shall overcome.

Let me remind us that it will not be easy. We have to work on, walk on, and pray on, with faith in our hearts. For the power of faith has sustained us, has enabled us to endure for generations. For you see, the hand that moves us is the hand that moves the world. Faith is the victory overcomes the world.

Let us pray . . .
Master, speak to your stewards;
Cause us to ever praise you and to
Acknowledge your plan in our lives.

Master, bend thy loving ear and listen this day;
Master, blot out all of the idle follies of today!
Master, should thou yet see fit to use this life of mine,
Master, help me work with Thee, and keep my hand in thine.
In the name of Jesus we pray—AMEN.

WE HAVE COME TOO FAR TO FORGET THE DREAM

Colonel Lindsey and members of the Red River Army Depot community, it is my pleasure to have been given the opportunity to join you in your observance of the life and accomplishments of the late Dr. Martin Luther King, Jr. You should know that I was particularly struck by your stated purpose in using this commemorative event as an occasion to focus on the accomplishments of Dr. King. Your ultimate objective to use this event as a vehicle toward strengthening the relationships between civilian and military personnel is a positive in your leadership.

As I am still serving in the U.S. Army Reserve as a commissioned officer, being among fellow soldiers makes this a very comfortable setting for me.

These occasions when organizations commemorate the life and circumstances of Dr. King are particularly meaningful to me. I say that because I had the privilege of living in the region where most of Dr. King's public activities were conducted. At the time of the Montgomery Bus Boycott, I was employed at Tuskegee Institute, a short 40 miles away from Montgomery. In fact, from the time of that important event until the untimely death of Dr. King, I resided in Tuskegee, Alabama. Therefore I could feel the tremors of his every action during those most eventful years. Really had an empty feeling when I went to my local barber on the evening when he was killed in Memphis.

On January 15, 1929, Martin Luther King, Jr. came into the world. He led the civil rights movement of the 60's and forced Americans to confront and pass judgment on their racial prejudices. Although the movement was truly popular, King was its catalyst and the undisputed prophet. Despite the early violent confrontations, miraculous changes occurred in a relatively short period of time.

The lunch counter, public school, city transit services, public accommodations, and the voting booth were all thrown open to Americans who had been heretofore excluded and without a voice. Away went the "colored" and "white only" signs. In fact, the days of separate accommodations vanished.

Without question, the vision of Dr. King changed America. As your theme for this program reflects, from that hot summer day on August 28, 1963, until this very moment, his electrifying "I Have a Dream" speech has remained alive and ever so relevant.

In the past four decades, the world has seen arise on three different continents, three great and strikingly similar men of peace. The lives of these three men have shown surprising parallels. Their philosophies have had remarkable influences, one upon the other. Their goals for humanity and their means of attaining those goals were alike. Striking, too, was the fact that they all preached non-violence, yet all died violent deaths. Two by assassin's bullets and the third by an accident still partially unexplained. These men and their works are now legends in our history.

Mahatma Gandhi, the Indian savant; Martin Luther King, Jr., the American civil rights leader whom we honor today; and Albert Luthuli, the South African nationalist chief and churchman.

Each of these men was living proof of the heavy loads of leadership. Each was proof of the truism associated with prophets being pilloried in their own lands. Yet, all three taught non-violence as the only practical means of opposing the overcoming unjust laws to restore human rights. Though all three were denigrated in their own lands, two of them—King and Luthuli—were accorded world recognition by receiving the Nobel Peace Prize. The third leader, Gandhi, might also have attained that prize had British colonial authorities in India had not feared him so.

Despite their geographic isolation, one from another; despite the great differences in their ages and backgrounds; despite the massive denigration of the work of each within his own land; there was an unusual juxtaposition of their aims, and an astonishing inter-mixture of tactics and goals. Thus, as they fought against differing tyrannies in different lands, they linked together in their principles, their philosophies, and their politics.

This historical fusion of the life and contributions of these individuals lends credence to your theme—"We've Come Too Far to Forget the Dream."

A brief historical journey can provide perspective for the occasion that we celebrate. By extraordinary historical coincidence, 1929 was the year that Gandhi delivered a message to the American Negro. It was also the year of the birth in Atlanta, Georgia of Martin Luther King, Jr. That newborn babe was destined to become the champion of civil rights in America, and of human dignity every where in the world. He was to follow closely Gandhi's techniques and torments. Like Gandhi, King was to die at the hands of an assassin. Like India's loss of Gandhi, America's loss of King's leadership would be suffered at a critical juncture in history.

King had been a firm protagonist of the thesis of non-violence of Gandhi. His defense of human dignity and his ability to inspire classes and masses might never have been called forth had he not been fully aware of Gandhi's tenets, and his political successes. For King, as for Gandhi, the man, the time, and the need, all converged at a crossroads of history.

Let me give you this short biographical sketch of Dr. King. His background and early life was unexceptional. His father was the pastor of a well-established Baptist church in Atlanta. King decided to follow in his father's footsteps as a clergyman. He pursued his college studies at Morehouse College in Atlanta. His graduate studies were at Crozier Seminary and Boston University where he earned his Ph.D.

He came to maturity with a rare combination of the physical and intellectual attributes of leadership. He possessed a broad humanitarian education, a forceful and dynamic personality, and a character of fortitude, courage and ambition. He had in addition, a magnificent oratorical voice. All these gifts of leadership his later life would demand.

King began digesting the philosophies of Gandhi as early as 1950. It was then that he literally became a disciple of the prophet, and began converting his principles into applicability in the American Negro's civil rights struggle. By so doing, King was destined to rekindle the philosophical fires of non-violence that burned in this country as a result of the writings of Henry Thoreau in the 19th century.

Association with and emphasis on he ideals of Gandhi found further motivation in the religious backgrounds of King and his black followers. What King did, one biographer records, was to turn the Negro faith in the church into a social movement. King united concepts of Gandhi and Christ with those of the devout Negro preachers. He overlaid these religious concepts with panoply of slogans and songs such as "We Shall Overcome."

These actions and symbols let loose black spirit and black pride. Additional fuel was fed these spiritual flames by the American white liberal establishment. It will be recalled that King's declared principle—"Stand up for righteousness, stand up for truth"—had also been the hallmark of Gandhi. In his writings, King subsequently stated that the spirit of the Montgomery Movement had come from Christ, the technique from Gandhi.

Though many have characterized him as a rebel, King was definitely not a revolutionary. He had a curious blend of pragmatism and idealism. He sought to build his movement upon constructive approaches and values. In his speeches and interviews, he usually focused on four themes: non-violence; constructive social change; individual and collective responsibility; and the price of freedom.

During the thirteen years of his public life he was fervent in his approach, yet consistent and courageous in seeking his goals. He seemed to take issue with Gandhi, however, on several of his courses of action. These he considered outside the bounds of legality. For example, he would not sanction strikes, or the disregard of civil authority, which had characterized certain of the Indian leader's drives. King's tactics were rather to bring public attention to the existence of unjust laws; but always within the existing constitutional framework.

During the course of his life, Martin Luther King, Jr. was the recipient of many honors. As he himself records, none pleased him more than the honorary degree from his own alma mater—Morehouse College in his hometown of Atlanta. In presenting the award, Morehouse College President Benjamin Mays said: "You are mature beyond your years; wiser at 28 than most men at 60; more courageous in a righteous struggle than most men will ever be; living a faith that most men preach about, but never experience."

A most profound, yet lucid interpretation of Gandhi's, of Luthuli's and King's goals is to be found in King's own words as he received the Nobel Peace Prize in 1964.

Said King, "I must ask why this prize is awarded to a movement which is beleaguered and committed to unrelenting struggle; to a movement which has not won the very peace and brotherhood which is the essence of the Nobel Prize. After contemplation, I can see that this award which I receive on behalf of the movement is a profound recognition—that non-violence is the answer to the crucial political and moral question of our time; the need for man to overcome oppression and violence without resorting to violence."

He continued with his acceptance with these words: "Civilization and violence are antithetical concepts. Negroes of the United States, following the people of India, have demonstrated that non-violence is not sterile passivity, but a powerful moral force, which makes for social transformation."

He then said, "Sooner or later, all the people of the world will have to discover a way to live together in peace. I accept this award today with an abiding faith in America, and an audacious faith in the future of mankind. I believe that what self-centered men have torn down, other-centered men can build up."

In concluding his acceptance speech, these words that have become classical reminders of Dr. King, uttered forth. "I am fully aware that this prize is much more than an honor to me personally; you honor the dedicated pilots of our struggle who sat at the controls as the freedom movement soared into orbit. I accept this honor and award in the spirit of a curator of some precious heirloom which he holds in trust for its true owners; all of those to whom beauty in truth resonates."

Our national administration has made it possible for us to recognize the contributions of Martin Luther King, Jr. with the observance of a national holiday. The federal holiday, which you at the Red River Depot will be celebrating, along with the rest of the nation, symbolizes (in the words of Mayor Andrew Young of Atlanta) "a nation committed at least by law and spirit to overcome the diversity of our population, and involve us together in a brotherhood and sisterhood of spirit. We should all know and realize that Martin Luther King's struggles continue in our nation and in us."

As I close, let me remind us of these profound words of Dr. King which were uttered very early in his public career, but repeated in the waning moments of that same public life. "I know that these are troubled times, but remember what I said to you in 1959—the ultimate measure of a man is not where he stands at times of comfort and convenience, but where he stands at times of challenge and controversy. The true neighbor will risk his position, his prestige, and even his life for the welfare of others. In dangerous valleys and hazardous pathways, he will lift some bruised and beaten brother to a higher and more noble life."

So, my friends, if we truly believe in the legacy that Dr. King left us, if we are holding fast to the premise that "We've Come Too Far to Forget the Dream," let us reach out and help one another. When we do that, and just that, the dream will be realized.

PART FIVE
End Notes

THOUGHTS ABOUT DR. KING AND MY DAD

Linda Jones, an educational writer, penned an article based on contributions from her father, Robert Jones, Jr. who was personally impacted by the life and death of Dr. King. In this article written a few years ago, she and her father remind us that though Dr. King was killed and his voice silenced, he lives on through countless, unnamed faces to whom he gave confidence and courage to speak.

"I'd like to do my part in observing the 40th anniversary of the assassination of Rev. Dr. Martin Luther King, Jr. by sharing what he meant to my father, Robert Jones, Jr. My father, who is 77 years old, lives in Akron, Ohio. He is a retired sanitation worker.

Dr. King was assassinated while he was in Memphis lending support to a sanitation worker's strike. Eight years ago while I was a writer for the Dallas Morning News, I interviewed my father for a story that I was writing about Dr. King. I wanted to hear what my father had to say about the man who made workers like him feel like they were somebody and sacrificed his life in the process. The article was written on January 17, 2000 and had the headline—Recollections of Martin Luther King—Civil rights leader's visits gave workers the courage to speak up for themselves."

Robert Jones, Jr. at Home in Akron, Ohio

"Whenever I think about Dr. Martin Luther King, Jr. and how he died, I am reminded of what my father did for a living. Robert Jones, Jr. held one of the most important, but least respected jobs in Akron, Ohio. He was a waste collector. The Rev. Dr. King was assassinated April 4, 1968, while in Memphis to lend support to people like Daddy."

"The Rev. King was in Memphis to speak on behalf of all sanitation workers who were striking for better wages, benefits and working conditions. It started out as a labor strike, but developed into a civil rights demonstration when the NAACP called for people to show support for the workers through acts of civil disobedience. Dr. King's appearance during the eight-week strike, where he led a protest march in March 1968, brought national attention to the workers' plight. He was killed the following month when he returned to lead a second march."

"I was sick over it," my father told me during a recent conversation. "I called Daddy because I wanted to know how he felt back then, when Dr. King went to Memphis to support workers like him who kept the city clean."

"He made a difference for us," my father said, shouting over the phone as our conversation transported his mind and his emotions back to those times."

"I'll tell it everywhere I go—and I'll say it loud. He lost his life trying to make it better for us and our conditions. We should honor Dr. King and his respect for 'little people.'"

The Rev. King's activities in Memphis lifted the spirits of my father and his black co-workers in Akron. It gave them a sense of dignity.

"He showed us that somebody cared about us. He helped make people stop looking at us like we were the lowest people in the world."

My father started working for the Akron city sanitation department in 1955 and stayed there for 30 years. I remember how he dutifully got up at dawn to report to work by 5 a.m., or earlier, to beat the summer heat. Every day he would meet the driver, mount the garbage truck and go on his rounds.

My father knew his job was important. My mother, my siblings and I were equally proud. But others didn't hold him or his co-workers in such high regard.

"They just down-graded us," he says. "There was no respect. But the minute we had a sit-down all those same people who were frowning their noses up were hollering because we were not picking up their mess."

Strangers, friends, even some family member's made fun of my father's occupation. But he took it in stride. It was an honest way to make a living and support his family.

But some comments were difficult to swallow—like the one made by a white foreman on the job. One of the black waste collectors questioned what appeared to be discriminatory hiring practices. The worker wanted to know why most of the garbage truck drivers were white, and why all of the collectors, who carried the waste buckets, were black.

"It's the white man's job to drive the truck and the black man's job to carry the garbage," the foreman told the worker.

He struggled to control his anger as he recalled those words.

"That's the way it went back then," my father told me. "They could get away with all of that and there was nothing we could do."

He said the men in his predominantly black department were overworked and underpaid. They were expected to cover large territories with faulty equipment. They got harassed by their supervisors. In later years, my father moved from being a waste collector to being a truck driver, but he had to pass more scrutiny than his white counterparts. He picked his battles and to keep his job, he uncharacteristically bit his tongue.

But the Rev. King's presence in Memphis was the morale boost my father said he needed to deal with the problems he and his co-workers were experiencing. It gave them the confidence and courage to speak their minds.

"Instead of complaining about ourselves, we started speaking loud," he said. "We were speaking like we weren't afraid anymore."

"What King did was the greatest thing in the world that could have happened for us," my father told me, but his final words about the man were laced with regret."

"I just hate that he lost his life over it,"

KING AND THE JEWS

By Clarence B. Jones

Earlier this month, at a Los Angeles event for the national African-American fraternity Kappa Alpha Psi, the keynote speaker launched into an anti-Semitic tirade—directed at the fraternity's guest of honor. The shocking episode shows just how far we've strayed from the original vision of the civil rights movement—and how far we have yet to travel to realize that vision.

The guest of honor, Daphna Ziman, an Israeli-American woman, who had just received the Tom Bradley Award for generous philanthropy and public service. But instead of praise, the Rev. Eric Lee berated her. "The Jews," he claimed, "have made money on in the music business and we are the entertainers, and they are economically enslaving us." (Mr. Lee would later apologize to Ms. Ziman.)

It was bad enough that the event took place on April 4, the 40th anniversary of Martin Luther King, Jr.'s assassination. Even more galling, Mr. Lee is the president-CEO of the L.A. branch of the Southern Christian Leadership Foundation—the very civil rights organization co-founded by the slain civil-rights leader.

Martin would have been repelled by Mr. Lee's remarks. I was his lawyer and one of his closest advisers, and I can say with absolute certainty that Martin abhorred anti-Semitism in all its forms, including anti-Zionism. "There isn't anyone in this country more likely to understand our struggle than Jews," Martin told me. "Whatever progress we've made so far as people, their support has been essential."

Martin was disheartened that so many blacks could be swayed by Elijah Muhammad's Nation of Islam and other black separatists, rejecting his message of non-violence, and grumbling about "Jew landlords" and "Jew interlopers"—even "Jew slave traders." The resentment and anger displayed toward people who offered so much support for civil rights was then nascent. But it has only festered and grown over four decades. Today, black-Jewish relations have arguably grown worse, not better.

For that, Martin would place fault principally on the shoulders of black leaders such as Louis Farrakhan, Al Sharpton and Jesse Jackson—either for making anti-Semitic statements, inciting anti-Semitism (including violence), or failing to condemn overt anti-Semitism within the black community.

When American cities were burning in the summers before he died, Martin listened to any number of young blacks holding matches blame Jewish landlords or Jewish store-owners in the inner-city—no matter that Jews were a minority of landlords and store owners. He asked them, "Who else might have bought the buildings that we lived in an rented us apartments? Where were these Negroes with money who'd abandoned their communities? And if blacks had bought those businesses and buildings, would they have charged less for rent and bread?"

As Martin wrote in 1967, "Negroes nurture a persistent myth that the Jews of America attained social mobility and status solely because they had money. It is unwise to ignore the error for many reasons. *In a negative sense it encourages anti-Semitism and over-estimates money as a value. In a positive sense, the full truth reveals a useful lesson.*

"Jews progressed because they possessed a tradition of education combined with social and political action. The Jewish family enthroned education and sacrificed to get it. The result was far more than abstract learning. Uniting social action with educational competence, Jews became enormously effective inn political life."

To Martin, who believed the pursuit of excellence would trump adversity; Jewish success should, and could, be used as a blueprint and inspiration for blacks' own success rather than as an incitement to bitterness.

Any blacks who subscribe to the views represented in Mr. Lee's speech would do well to heed the word and deeds of the man whose name and legacy they claim to represent.

Mr. Jones was Martin Luther King's personal attorney and close adviser. He is the co-author, with Joel Engel, of "What Would Martin Say" (Harper, 2008), from which this article was adapted. The article first appeared in the Wall Street Journal.

MARTIN LUTHER KING, JR.'S REAL DREAM:

BLACK SELF-EMPOWERMENT

Gordon Jackson
The Dallas Weekly

Dr. Martin Luther King, Jr.'s final annual report to the SCLC revealed the main thrust of his vision for Black America. Less than a year later, he was slain.

It's a no-brainer that Dr. Martin Luther King, Jr. had a dream. He spoke about it in what became one of the greatest speeches in the history of mankind, his "I Have a Dream" speech August 23, 1963, during the March on Washington. If not before then, that moment thrust him well into the mainstream spotlight. As his national holiday returns, this year observing his 75th birthday, it will reflect on how he won the hearts and admiration of all people, regardless of race, color, religion and gender.

Today, however, in 2004, Black America is still trying to "overcome." Yes, much progress had been made, but many of the same issues that plagued the community back in King's days still exist. This past year, we saw continuous attacks on affirmative action in both the workforce and education arena, more negative portrayal of blacks proportionately by the mainstream media, glaring health disparities between blacks and whites, alleged racial profiling and police brutality cases ongoing and the passing of a controversial power-grabbing mid-decade redistricting bill that targeted blacks and Hispanics.

What seems to be compounding such barriers is what some feel is a complacent and unmotivated black community, focusing more on social matters, or in today's terms "bling bling" thinking that the community has arrived. That bodes the question of it Black America has lost sight of Dr. King's dream. The answer to that may be "yes," especially when you deeply study the hard-core components of his vision. Some may have missed that, underneath the feeling-good bright and shining image of global harmony surrounding MLK are the real makings of what he was striving for: black self-empowerment.

Perhaps the most telling indication of Dr. King's mindset, particularly during the last year of his life was on August 16, 1967, in Atlanta, when he delivered the Annual Report for the Southern Christian Leadership Conference.

Giving a sense of how times were for blacks 10 years before, King reported:

"Ten years ago, legislative halls of the South were still ringing loud with such words as 'interposition' and 'nullification.' All types of conniving methods were still being used to keep the Negro from becoming a registered voter. A decade ago, not a single Negro entered the legislative chambers of the South except as a porter of chauffer. Ten years ago, all too many Negroes were still harried by day and haunted by night by a corroding sense of fear and a nagging sense of nobody-ness."

King spoke of how, first, Black America needed to be liberated mentally before they had any hopes of freeing themselves literally:

"In this decade of change, the Negro stood up and confronted his oppressor. He faced the bullies and the guns, and the dogs and the tear gas. He put himself squarely before the vicious mobs and moved with strength and dignity toward them and decisively defeated them. And the courage with which he confronted enraged mobs dissolved the stereotype of the grinning, submissive Uncle Tom. He came out of his struggle integrated only slightly in the external society, but powerfully integrated within. This was a victory that had to precede all other gains.

In short, over the last ten years the Negro decided to straighten his back up, realizing that a man cannot ride your back unless it is bent. We made our government write new laws to alter some of the cruelest injustices that affected us. We made an indifferent and unconcerned nation rise from lethargy and subpoenaed its conscience to appear before the judgment seat of morality on the whole question of civil rights. We gained manhood in the nation that had always called us 'boy.'"

King's report on the achievements of the SCLC program Operation Breadbasket clearly indicated how the organization focused hard on producing new jobs and increasing new income for the black community:

"...we have achieved for the Negro community of Chicago more than twenty-two hundred new jobs with an income of approximately eighteen million dollars a year, new income for the Negro community."

He further spoke of SCLC's work in nurturing black-owned banks, in lieu of trying to win over participation from white owned financial institutions:

"... there was another area through this economic program, and that was the development of financial institutions which were controlled by Negroes and which were sensitive to problems of economic deprivation of the Negro community. The two banks in Chicago that were interested in helping Negro businessmen were largely unable to loan much because of limited assets. Hi-Lo, one of the chair stores in Chicago, agreed to maintain substantial accounts in the two banks, thus increasing their ability to serve the needs of the Negro community . . . as both of these Negro-operated banks have now more than double their assets, and this has been done in less than a year by the work of Operation Breadbasket."

A similar initiative in Cleveland led to the city's top major dairy company to hire more "Negroes," advertise in "Negro newspapers" and deposit more funds in "Negro financial institutions." At one point, when Sealtest resisted from cooperating, King responded in consistency with his non-violent philosophy:

"Mr. Sealtest, we're sorry. We aren't going to burn your store down. We aren't going to throw any bricks in the window. But we are going to put picket signs around and we are going to put leaflets out and we are going to our pulpits and tell them not to sell Sealtest products, and not to purchase Sealtest products."

It worked. They also convinced A&P, the city's top grocery store chain at the time to pull Sealtest products off their shelves in the whole city, not just in the black neighborhoods. Sealtest signed the agreement, resulting in about half a million more dollars ($2.7 million in today's dollars) being pumped into the black community.

In the field of housing, King and SCLC, were making strides there as well. They and his church, Ebenezer Baptist Church, had completed plans to build 152 units of low-income housing for seniors in downtown Atlanta. They had also laid out plans for more of the same "from Mississippi to North Carolina, using Negro workmen, Negro architects, Negro attorneys and Negro financial institutions throughout." They grasped hopes of building up to $40 million ($219.7 million in today's dollars) of new housing for blacks.

In his report, the brilliant King gave detailed accounts of how African Americans had been historically deprived in terms of education, healthcare and economics by the white establishment. He also spoke of how blacks were affected psychologically:

"Even semantics have conspired to make that which is black seem ugly and degrading. (Yes) in Roget's Thesaurus there are some 120 synonyms for blackness and at least sixty of them are offensive, such words as blot, soot, grime, devil, and foul. And there are 134 synonyms for whiteness and all are favorable, expressed in such words as purity, cleanliness, chastity, and innocence. A white lie is better than a black lie. The most degenerate member of a family is the 'black sheep.' Ossie Davis has suggested that maybe the English language should be reconstructed so that teachers will not be forced to teach the Negro child sixty ways to despise himself and thereby perpetuate his false sense of inferiority, and the white child 134 ways to adore himself, and thereby perpetuate his false sense of superiority. The tendency to ignore the Negro's contribution to American life and strip him of his personhood is as old as the earliest history books and as contemporary as the morning's newspaper.

While King publicly denounced the 'Black Power' cry that was coined by black activists Stokely Carmichael and Willie "Mukassa" Ricks, that didn't mean he stood against a form of acquiring black pride. He stated:

"To offset this cultural homicide, the Negro must rise up with an affirmation of his own Olympian manhood. Any movement of the Negro's freedom that overlooks this necessity is only waiting to be buried. As long as the mind is enslaved, the body can never be free. Psychological freedom, a firm sense of self-esteem, is the most powerful weapon against the long night of physical slavery. No Lincolnian Emancipation Proclamation, no Johnsonian civil rights bill can totally bring this kind of freedom. The Negro will only be free when he reaches down to the inner depths of his own being and signs with the pen and ink of assertive manhood his own emancipation proclamation. And with a spirit straining toward true self-esteem, the Negro must boldly throw off the manacles of self-abnegation and say to himself and to the world, 'I am somebody.'"

Dr. King then went further into the need for blacks to organize their economic and political clout. Making his speech before several ministers, he took a position on the spiritual viewpoint of having power, saying that there was nothing wrong with it if used correctly. He added:

"Now what has happened is that we've had it wrong and mixed up in our country, and this has led Negro Americans in the past to seek their goals through love and moral suasion devoid of power, and white Americans to seek their goals through power devoid of love and conscience. It is leading a few extremists today to advocate for Negroes the same destructive and conscienceless power that they have justly abhorred in whites. It is precisely this collision of immoral power with powerless morality which constitutes the major crisis of our times."

As King was assessing solutions to the issues mentioned, he said:

"The problem indicates that our emphasis must be twofold: We must create full employment, or we must create incomes. People must be made consumers by one method or the other. Once they are placed in this position, we need to be concerned that the potential of the individual is not wasted. New forms of work that enhance the social good will have to be devised for those for whom traditional jobs are not available."

His following statement indicated that King did not wish for the black family to conform to poverty, giving his vision of how a healthy family is also a financially secure and independent one.

"Beyond these advantages, a host of positive psychological changes will inevitably result from widespread economic security. The dignity of the individual will flourish when the decisions concerning his life are in his own hands, when he has the assurance that his income is stable and certain, and when he knows that he has the means to seek self-improvement. Personal conflicts between husband, wife, and children will diminish when the unjust measurement of human worth on a scale of dollars is eliminated."

King reaffirmed his stand on nonviolent strategies, in comparison to the series of race riots that had taken place over the decade. He assessed that rioting was non-productive in helping the black community make any significant gains:

"At best, the riots have produced little additional anti-poverty money allotted by frightened government officials and a few water sprinklers to cool the children of the ghettos. It is something like improving the food in the prison while the people remain securely incarcerated behind bars. Nowhere have the riots won any concrete improvement such as have the organized protest demonstrations."

He put a stamp on his position by saying:

"This is no time for romantic illusions and empty philosophical debates about freedom. This is a time for action. What is needed is a strategy for change, a tactical program that will bring the Negro into the mainstream of American life as quickly as possible. So far, the nonviolent movement has only offered this. Without recognizing this we will end up with solutions that don't solve, answers that don't answer, and explanations that don't explain."

Dr. King wrapped up his annual report address in similar manner to his "I Have a Dream" speech, making bullet points on his vision.

> "Let us be dissatisfied until the tragic walls that separate the outer city of wealth and comfort from the inner city of poverty and despair shall be crushed by the battering rams of the forces of justice."

> "Let us be dissatisfied until those who live on the outskirts of hope are brought into the metropolis of daily security."

> "Let us be dissatisfied until slums are cast into the junk heaps of history and every family will live in a decent, sanitary home."

> "Let us be dissatisfied until the dark yesterdays of segregated schools will be transformed into bright tomorrows of quality integrated education."

> "Let us be dissatisfied until integration is not seen as a problem but as an opportunity to participate in the beauty of diversity."

"Let us be dissatisfied until that day when nobody will shout, 'White Power!' when nobody will shout, 'Black Power!' but everybody will talk about God's power and human power."

On April 4, 1968, less than eight months after his last annual report to the SCLC, Dr. Martin Luther King, Jr. was assassinated. Most of his plans and vision of concrete black self-determination seemed to have died with him.

What would have been the ultimate answer for King? To nurture and grow the nation's black colleges, as opposed to gaining entry into white colleges? To establish black-owned multi-million dollar black corporations, compared to breaking into management with white companies? To build black-owned banks and financial institutions, as opposed to seeing support from white-owned banks.

For King, it wasn't one extreme or the other, but a balanced medium. Yet, according to excerpts of some of his other speeches, there's one thing for sure; he did not abandon the black community. He didn't lose sight of hard-core Black America, while building relationships with aspects of the white community. He had become mainstream, but not while defecting the black community.

King used his fame and influence to better conditions for black folks, for he truly visioned a progressive, proud and vibrant black community. That also was his true dream.

Note: The final annual report of Dr. Martin Luther King, Jr. to the Southern Christian Leadership Conference is one of the most powerful presentations of Dr. King. It is my opinion that he should also be accorded prominence as we reflect on the life of Dr. King, and as we seek to "realize the dream." My *thanks to my friend and associate Gordon Jackson for his permission to use his article in the publication.*

CELEBRATING MARTIN
Bernice Powell Jackson
The Dallas Weekly

This year, as we approach his birthday, it is especially important to remember an often forgotten side of the modern-day prophet Martin Luther King, Jr. So many Americans know him only by his 1963 March on Washington speech and his image of a little black child and a little white child holding hands in a free nation. Others know only of his commitment to non-violence as a means of resistance, a commitment that led to his being awarded the Nobel Peace Prize.

But in the last year or so of his life Dr. King found himself challenging this nation on a very different subject—our participation in an unjust war. As a result, even many of his friends and supporters turned their back on him. Was it out of fear or a sense of patriotism, or out of the belief that he was abandoning his commitment to working for racial justice?

What they did not comprehend was that Dr. King understood in the depths of his soul that the quest for justice and the quest for peace are inextricably entwined.

"When machines and computers, profit motives and property rights are considered more important than people, the giant triplets of racism, materialism and militarism are incapable of

being conquered," said Dr. King at the Riverside Church in New York City exactly a year before his assassination. Later that year the Canadian Broadcasting System aired a series of lectures by Dr. King on the same theme. In one of them he answered those who asked if he wasn't a civil rights movement leader, thereby trying to exclude him from the peace movement, by saying, "I have worked too long and hard now against segregated public accommodations to end up segregating my moral concern," adding, "Justice is indivisible."

He also explained, "It must be said it would be rather absurd to work passionately and unrelentingly for integrated schools and not be concerned about the survival of a world in which to be integrated."

In his Riverside Church sermon, Dr. King also explained his call for an end to the Vietnam War by reminding his listeners of his commission to continue to work for peace as a recipient of the Nobel Peace Prize.

Moreover, he spoke of his call to Christian ministry. "To me the relationship of this ministry to the making of peace is so obvious that I sometimes marvel at those who ask me why I am speaking against the war. Have they forgotten that my ministry is in obedience to the one who loved his enemies so fully that he died for them?"

Dr. King saw his call to the nation to wage peace instead of war as both a privilege and a burden, but he said, "We are called to speak for the weak, for the voiceless, for the victims of our nation and for those it calls enemy, for no document from human hands can make these humans any less our brothers." His words are just as true today as they were nearly four decades ago.

For Dr. King, non-violence was a way of life. It was a commitment beyond all others. It meant that injustice and evil must be confronted, but not with war or violence. That is a truism that all too often is forgotten in the rush to arms and our tendency to cast the "enemy" as less than human.

In the words of the 2002 Nobel Peace laureate, President Jimmy Carter, "War may sometimes be a necessary evil. But no matter how necessary, it always is an evil, never a good. We will not learn how to live together in peace by killing each other's children."

This year, as we celebrate Dr. King's birthday—let's do something for peace. Let's march. Let's pray. Let's write our President and Congress. Let's hold candlelight vigils. Let's ring our federal buildings with signs for peace.

To work for peace would honor Dr. King.

Note: The inclusion of this column by Bernice Powell Jackson is timely in that it addresses an area of Dr. King's life and work that is not accorded much attention with the passage of time.

A LASTING REMINDER

As this collection of messages and thoughts were designed to chronicle the life and legacy of Dr. Martin Luther King, Jr., there is a final thought that should be included. If not included, this development and his life and contributions could fade out of our memories.

Twenty-five years after the assassination of Dr. Martin Luther King, Jr., Memphis Circuit Court judge D'Army Bailey and five other Black community leaders rescued the Lorraine Motel from a foreclosure sale in 1982 and converted it into a museum.

Dr. King is a special feature in the museum, but he is not the focal point. The museum commemorates many people who led up to and were involved in the civil rights movement. It is not a memorial to Dr. King, but to all who participated in the movement. The executive director says, "There were a lot of people—not rich or famous, but common people—with tenacity and courage to fight the system and bring about a change."

One of the residents of the Lorraine Motel in the 1950s and early 1960s had this to say about the museum: "The museum is a good tool to teach young people about how things were in this country. I know history and culture are to a people as water is to a fish. They're everything. If we don't have that history and the culture that comes out of it, we will continue to be a people who are at the footstool of every other civilization on the planet."

Calvin Brown lived at the Lorraine Hotel from 1972 until 1988, and is said to be the oldest living resident of the facility. He had this quote in an article that appeared in a Memphis weekly paper: "The Lorraine was the Calvary of the civil rights movement and should be preserved as a historic site."

The writer also said: "There is no other facility like it. It is a reflection of a lot of hard work by a lot of people."

Hopefully if a reader of this collection happens to be in Memphis, Tennessee at some point in the future, you may wish to stop and visit the Lorraine Hotel Museum.

CELEBRATING THE DREAM OF DR. MARTIN LUTHER KING, JR.

We obviously have not achieved Dr. King's dreams because there is still inequality and divisiveness among the races. Although there are not as many blatant examples of hate crimes and brutality, some would argue that our situation is worse now because the racism we must deal with today is institutional, which is more dangerous and more difficult to combat because it is often indiscernible. Thus, the prejudice that Dr. King fought to eradicate has not improved; it has merely morphed, having taken on newer, stronger forms.

There are still many issues that deserve our attention. Incidents of police brutality, stripping blacks of their voting rights, inadequate materials and facilities at black schools; and yet the outrage of our predecessors does not seem to be reflected today. We seem to be saying, "If it doesn't affect me as a person, then I'm not worried about it."

This is not what Dr. King would have wanted. For him, the struggle belonged to all of us, not just blacks, but everyone. And the fact that his own people seem to be ignoring the problems that plague their community, would undoubtedly disappoint him.

Tensions within the black race do not seem to have improved much either. Contention based on differences in class, education and skin pigmentation are as pervasive as ever. Yet, the various groups believe that they are truly an embodiment of what's "real," of how blacks should be. What we fail to realize is there were no conditions on Dr. King's dream. He never said, "We shall overcome . . . but only if we're all middle class and above." His vision was not only promised to those who possess high levels of melanin in their skin, or those who choose to wear natural hairstyles, braids, and corn row perms.

All this is not to say that there have not been improvements in the past 40 plus years. Blacks do have more career and educational opportunities and social freedoms than we have ever had before. Many have taken advantage of these opportunities and opened doors for others. We have African-Americans in positions of power in sports, politics, entertainment, Fortune 500 companies, and, yes, even in all sectors of education. Some of those who have risen have directed their money and influence toward noble causes for the "greater good."

P. Diddy's 2004 "Vote or Die" campaign aimed at minority voters, which despite his efforts, did not result in increased youth presence at the polls. Magic Johnson is another example of an individual who should be commended for his commitment to strengthening the community by establishing black-owned businesses in predominantly black areas across the nation.

As we celebrate the life and legacy of a great human being who stood for peace, equality and justice, we should take the time to reflect upon how far we came; where we are now; and the distance we must travel to reach that "not so impossible dream."

WE NEED TO RE-DREAM THE DREAM

January 15, 2008 marked the 79th birthday of Dr. Martin Luther King, Jr., and we still struggling with "the dream." Persistent recurrences of racial incidents continue to engage the American consciousness with the question of race. The 1992 riots in the wake of the verdict in the Rodney King beating trial were the first signs of fracturing. Varying reactions to the O.J. Simpson trial verdicts revealed the differences in perspective that black and white Americans generally possess. Both cases stirred anger and resentment across racial lines. Tensions continue, and weekly (if not daily) we hear of yet another incident somewhere in our country where race is presented as a precipitating factor. The question has to be asked, are we still living the dream?

In the wake of the civil rights movement in which Dr. King was so intensely involved, there came a flood of social programs that sought to address the causes and consequences of racism. Cultural education, cross cultural dialogue, and the current multi-cultural initiatives, all hearken back to the civil rights movement for their mandates.

In the pursuit of the rights of various groups under the civil rights umbrella, one thing has become clear. That which was called right by one group is often called wrong by another. Rather than resolving the differences, tolerance is championed as the appropriate response to the varying perspectives that have emerged. Yet, tolerance has no cohesive or healing power in society. It means little more than leaving one another alone. It leads to indifference, not understanding. Tolerance allows the gulfs between us to remain place. In fact, there is little in the concept of tolerance to pull us away from racial isolation.

Tolerance brings with it an implicit moral relativism. Who is to say what is right and what is wrong. Moral relativism suggests that there are no absolutes to which we can all be held accountable. Such a thing was far from the thinking of Dr. Martin Luther King, Jr.

Dr. King did not speak in terms of tolerance. His ideal was love. Yet, in current discussions of race relations the word love is seldom mentioned. Dr. King insisted love was the dominant or critical value by which we could overcome racial strife. The love he spoke of was a biblical love, one that is unconditional, unselfish, and seeks the absolute good of another party. The kind of love is a tough love, one that confronts wrong and injustice with the truth—absolute truth as decreed by an all powerful God and enables the individual to love their enemy. The civil rights struggle has now become the staff of nostalgia, history books, and the memoirs of aging former civil rights leaders. Yet, millions remain in poverty, and racial discrimination that still pervades much of American society.

Dr. King's vision of what America still can be continues to challenge us to do our part to make that vision a reality for millions of Americans of all races. He spoke passionately about the need for racial harmony around the world. Let him not be the last to speak of it. Dr. King believed that the greatest tragedy of his period was not the noise of the "bad" people, but the appalling silence of the so-called good people. Our responsibility now is to break the silence and re-dream Dr. King's dream.

We are still judging people by the color of their skin, the shape of their body, their gender, their ethnicity—all of which are irrelevant to a parson's character. There are ongoing violent conflicts around the world based on prejudice and hatred. In this country, a Black man was dragged to his death behind a pickup truck in Jasper, Texas. A young gay college student was brutally beaten and left for dead, hanging on a barbed wire fence. Just two incidents of modern day lynching that occurred out of hatred and prejudice.

We have a lot of work to do and we should get better at it, because the dream could turn into a nightmare. The good news is that hatred and prejudice are not genetic. Racism, chauvinism, bigotry are learned and reinforced socially and politically. What is learned can be unlearned. And we could just stop teaching it.

There is a need to re-dream the dream.

Second Annual City-Wide
M.L. King Observance
Schenectady County Inner-City Ministries
Schenectady Human Relations Commission
Schenectady, New York
February 1988

A DREAM STILL TO BE REALIZED

It is nearly twenty-five years since a national civil-rights revolution was launched by King's eloquent dream, and the palpable witness of a quarter of a million marchers at the Lincoln Memorial. But still, it is a dream deferred in many ways.

The Rev. Dr. Martin Luther King, Jr. never held a public office or amassed great wealth and he was often vilified during his thirteen years in the public eye. But his biblically based appeal for racial equality, justice and brotherhood inspired a social and political movement that changed America.

From the anti-segregation protests in Montgomery, Alabama thirty-three years ago, to his assassination in Memphis in 1968, King, who would have been 59 last Friday, blazed a freedom trail that has made him one of the revered figures of the 20th century.

So it is appropriate that Dr. Martin Luther King's birthday is now celebrated as a national holiday along with that of George Washington and Abraham Lincoln. All three are figures in American history whose personal drive, vision and ability propelled them to pivotal roles in epochs which shaped the future course of the nation.

George Washington is universally revered for his leadership in the Revolutionary War and his role in inventing the Constitution and the Presidency. Abraham Lincoln, the poor farm boy who became president, ensured the preservation of America as a land of liberty and justice for all.

The Rev. Dr. Martin Luther King, Jr. worked in the fulcrum of one of the nation's most tumultuous decades. He led a movement to cleanse America of a tragic and nearly fatal fault. It is for that reason that we observed a national holiday this past Monday.

Twenty years ago, an assassin's bullet sliced through the chill Memphis air and ended Dr. King's life. That act brought to a close an era which rivaled "King's work challenged Americans to examine their beliefs and compare them to the realities of American life. Could a "land of the free" legally disenfranchise 20 percent of its population? Could "on nation under God" live with separate schools, separate facilities, and separate opportunities for blacks and whites, and still call itself one nation?

The answer was a resounding no! The result was civil legislation to enfranchise all Americans and open the day to the good life for everyone, including those who needed a safety net to survive. It also led to an anti-war movement—in which Dr. King was deeply involved.

This is the second year in which Dr. King has been honored with a national holiday. It seems somehow wrong that we, as a nation, must be reminded of him while Americans automatically bake the cherry pies for Washington's Birthday, and pull out the Gettysburg Address for the birthday of Lincoln. Perhaps it takes time to create a memory with the metaphorical force of Mt.

Rushmore. Washington has the jump of 200 years over Dr. King, and Lincoln has an advantage of almost 130 years.

The day will come when Dr. King who, had he lived, would still be considered a young man, will have the same historical importance as they. And then American citizens will need no reminders of his birthday, nor any justification for it. It is for that reason that we must conclude that his dream has not yet been realized. Dr. King has a firm foothold in history. He has earned a place with the titans of this nation and the gratitude of those who lived through this era of change, and those who were born into the America he helped create. But his dream has not yet been realized. Has it been deferred? Is it being denied?

Dr. King said that "America is essentially a dream, a dream as yet fulfilled. It is a dream of a land where men of all races, of all nationalities and of all creeds can live together as brothers." He continued—"One of the first things we notice in this dream is an amazing universalism. It does not say some men, but says all men. It does not say white men but says all men, which includes black men. It does not say all Gentiles, but says all men which includes Jews. It does not say all Protestants, but says all men, which includes Catholics."

The American dream reminds us that every man is heir to the legacy of worthiness. The highest honor we can give him is to work to make his dreams come. Too often on occasions such as this, we expect the speaker to deliver a polite short talk. Toy around the edges of the theme, but don't hold the audience too long. I promise you that I will not tarry here long. Yet, if we are to work to make his dream come true—come alive, we must spend time working in the vineyard. We must work to ensure that we do not lose touch with what caused him to become a drum major for justice and decency. Racial harmony has not arrived for all of God's children. In spite of what happened in Montgomery, Washington and Memphis, we are not there yet.

Therefore, let me spend just a few moments reminiscing about my youth in the segregated south in Mississippi. It's not dwell on the bitterness of the past, but to draw from that experience some insights that can be used to deal with our problems today. For while he laws and customs of America has changed, poverty, diminished opportunity, and racism continue.

Growing up black in Mississippi taught you a lot. It taught you that you did not have the same rights white people had. That if you rode a bus it had to be under a sign that said "colored." That going downtown was inconvenient at best, and dangerous at worst. Moreover, that poverty had an extra, black dimension to it. You learned that poverty and racism had the potential to grind people down—drain them of energy and creativity—damage their self-esteem and hopes.

But those of the era survived, and so did many of today's businessmen, doctors, lawyers, educators and public servants who grew up poor and segregated. We knew that we had to be better in order to get ahead, and we competed hard against one another, but on strictly friendly terms.

And there was a fourth factor too, which was work. Even small children did odd jobs. Delivering newspapers, watering lawns, cleaning up yards, and running errands. I earned my first dollar in the cotton fields of Mississippi as my grandmother taught me and my little brother how to chop cotton and carry pails of water to the field workers. I recall how my little chest stuck out when I showed my mother my first day's wages. When I gave the money to her to "hold for me." When I gave her half of my first week's earnings. When I purchased my first wrist watch—a wire, expansion band model. How proud I was!

How proud was I when my father told me that he wanted his sons to work, but not in the cotton fields. How proud was I when he made work for us on his private construction jobs. My father was, and still is, a proud man and I have tried to be "just like him." Unfortunately, many of today's youth do not have such opportunities. They can't get out to the suburban malls where the jobs have moved. The ghetto economy is stagnant, with only one job for every twenty kids.

Times have changed since my young days in Mississippi. Conditions have changed. In the past, poor kids had role models in the black businessmen and professionals who lived next door, or around the corner, or down the street. Today they see them only on weekends, when concerned and successful black people drive in to do volunteer work. But they quickly leave when the volunteer stint is finished. In the past, our neighborhoods had greater cohesion and enforced a value structure that helped to break the cycle of poverty.

Today we see people trying valiantly to do the same, but too often they are overwhelmed by the plague of drugs and crime that corrodes their lives. And then there are the callous bureaucrats and exploiters who weaken their neighborhood-building efforts.

In the past, our schools believed in our kids, taught them pride and the skills they needed to get ahead. Today, too many of our kids are in schools that don't trust them, don't believe in them, and don't care about them.

In the past, we had opportunities to work at low-skill jobs that taught u us habits of responsibility that we carried into our adult lives. Today most black and poor kids can't find those jobs. Teenage unemployment is over 50 percent in many urban cities for black kids—and neither can their parents find work.

In the past we encountered a racism that was demeaning and brutal. But today's racism may be even more insidious. Then, we knew the enemy and he flaunted his power and his hatred. Today's racism comes in brighter packages of smiles, nods and unspoken stereotypes. But we must not forget that racism is racism, no matter how it may be wrapped.

The most important subject young people need to be taught about today isn't found in any textbook—does not requires a computer to be put into practice—and can't be measured by any standardized test. The subject is bigotry. Some call it bigotry; others prejudice; other racism. Still others call is discrimination. Many believe that it is a natural part of life, even in this, the most democratic society on earth.

Sadly, in a society celebrating the 200th anniversary of he most important document of freedom in history, we are still witnessing blatant evidences of prejudice and bigotry and racism. And it is mounted against African-Americans, Jews, Hispanics, Asians, women, the elderly and others. Is the dream of Dr. King still alive?

So while we may speak of the strengths and the persistence and perseverance of generations of black folk, we have to recognize that in spite of all the progress we have made, masses of our brothers and sisters are still victimized by racism. They are still mired in poverty. They are still held down by situations that must be changed. Is the dream of Dr. King still alive?

Racial bigotry is insidious, often so subtle that we are unaware of our own unspoken prejudice. When we are not directly confronted by its unjust, sometimes brutal results in our daily lives, complacency allows us to take refuge in the all too comforting lie that racial harmony has virtually been achieved.

There are some who are deeply disturbed by their own lingering prejudice, and they know that they need all of the help they can get to confront and deal with it. For these reasons, those same individuals look to the religious leaders whom they respect for guidance and counsel in their daily struggle, to internalize the theoretical concepts of racial harmony and peace.

That is the kind of leadership that Dr. King provided in his tragically short life, and so much more. Behind the magnificent words—"I have a dream"—was his understanding that prejudice and bigotry linger in the irrational, dark recesses of the human mind and cannot be excised immediately or easily.

Racial intolerance and its effects must, rather, be confronted every day in a thousand small ways before the final victory of justice and equality is ultimately won. This cannot, however, excuse complacency, inaction and silence. Sins of omission are just as harmful as sins of commission. The incidents involving Howard Beach, Jimmy "The Greek" Snyder, and similar situations show that we have a long way to travel to achieve the racial harmony and peace for which congregations prayed, and Dr. King lived and fought for. It also shows that our words, as well as our silence, and our actions don't quite match our noble, abstract intentions.

Twenty-five years after the march on Washington, two decades after his brutal assassination, King's legacy still challenges us to keep faith with our God and our own better nature. As hard as that be to do, not one of us has a legitimate excuse to do less.

John Jacob in an address before he Houston Urban League made the forceful point that Americans are beginning to understand that their fates are linked. He used the term, "the great thaw." The "great thaw" is coming because Americans are learning that we can't be comfortable with someone else's misery. We must care about the hungry, the homeless, or the unemployed. They cannot be ignored just because we happen to be well-fed, well-housed, and have jobs.

Public opinion polls now show that Americans reject further cuts in social programs. They want more done to solve our social problems. The polls show blacks and whites in agreement about basic issues t a greater degree than ever before. We see the revival of conscience and fairness in the call for full employment and social justice by the National Conference of Catholic Bishops. And we see it in the massive anti-apartheid sentiment that forced a change in national policies toward South Africa.

But, again according to John Jacob, a thaw won't be enough. America needs a great awakening to fulfill the promise of justice and equality. To revitalize our economy to provide jobs and opportunity. To integrate minorities into the mainstream of society.

The civil rights movement, that received its contemporary impetus from Dr. King, has been attacked for dwelling on society's imperfections and ignoring the progress of an oppressed people is the result of our concern with society's failings. Together we must work to help move our society forward by continuing to identify what's wrong and how best to fix it.

Civil rights advocacy and human rights advocacy, in the remainder of the 80's and beyond, has to continue to deal with economic issues. Because more blacks and other minorities have lost their jobs through industrial decline than through job discrimination.

And we need to have crime, health, housing, education and other issues on our agenda as well. Crack, heroin, cocaine, poor health care, lack of affordable housing, and inferior schools ruin more black lives that the Ku Klux Klan ever did.

Today, black organizations must press ahead with those issues if we are to play our role in hastening America's Great Awakening. We must also be reminded, all of us, that there will be no Great Awakening while racism is still alive and well. Is the dream deferred? Delayed? Denied?

As a nation we have stopped investing inn people, and especially in your people at risk. All the talk about making America competitive again is nonsense without a massive commitment to educate and train our young people—beginning with the poorest, the most vulnerable, and the most at risk.

In my state of Texas, studies show that an investment of less than $2 billion in preventing dropouts and increasing college attendance would yield almost $18 billion in higher wages and tax revenues, and lower crime and welfare costs.

Nor can the dream be realized without aggressive policies that meet the urgent health, housing and survival needs of the poorest among us. Families aren't homeless today because they like sleeping in parks or shelters, or over heating grates. They are homeless because the government and the private sector have stopped building low-income housing. There is also the issue of so few people get Medicaid or welfare assistance.

The private sector has to be part of the realization of the Dream also. It needs to do more to move minorities up the corporate ladder, and to start doing more of what it claims to do—create jobs. Last year American industry spent more of its capital on mergers than it did on research and development, and the capital investment that creates jobs and wins markets in the growing global economy.

Therefore, groups like you assembled here, must unite to cause our government and the private sector, as well as citizen groups, to focus attention on making America competitive in the long run. There must be a concentrated focus on creating a new social bond that unites us all. A bond that builds partnerships that work to end poverty, create jobs, and usher in a new era of prosperity and brotherhood.

Yu ask—is this an illusion? No more an illusion than the ides that brought the Founders of this nation to Philadelphia 200 years ago to construct a new nation and a Constitution to govern it.

Unfortunately, they created a flawed structure. A structure that tolerated slavery. A structure that defined blacks as three-fifths of other Americans. A structure that became democratic through the pain of civil war and reconstruction, and in the fitful, periodic drives to reform and renew our society.

Dr. King took us to the point where we, all of us, could come to understand that it was possible to dream. Through his leadership this nation went through an important period of renewal. We may be nearing another one of those cycles of renewal, a period in which Americans will once again recover the spirit that fights the racism and poverty that stain our democracy.

That spirit did not die with the tragic death of Dr. King. That spirit has not died in what is now termed the "Ice Age." It's a spirit that goes far back in our history—right to the very beginnings when we had our flawed revolution.

It is a spirit that is shared by all decent people, regardless of color or national origin. It's a spirit of protest and faith. It is the spirit that lad Black Texans to celebrate Juneteenth as the real Independence Day.

It is the spirit of Frederick Douglass who told us that "If there is n struggle there is no progress." It is the spirit of W.E.B. DuBois, who told us that "Black people demand equality. Political equality, industrial equality, and social equality, and we should never rest until we achieve it."

It is the spirit of Whitney Young, who gave us this vision of the future. "It is the vision of an America in which children don't go hungry because their skin is black—an America in which mothers don't go homeless because their skin happens to be black.

It is a vision of an America which provides its people with choices and with the means to exercise them. It is a vision of an America which glorifies in is diversity and respects the unique contributions and traditions of all it's people."

Young said "the open society will come about when all decent people, both black and white, are galvanized to change the present society."

It is also a spirit captured in these words of Dr. King: ", , , many of our white brothers, as evidenced by their presence here today, have come to realize that their destiny is tied up in our destiny. And they have come to realize that their freedom is inextricably bound to our freedom. We cannot walk alone."

Yes, my friends, we truly cannot walk alone if we want the dream of Dr. King to be realized. Therefore, let us, together work to lay the foundation for a Great Revival that brings Whitney Young's "Open Society" into existence.

Let us bring whites and blacks and brown together to work for the changes that Dr. King lived and died for. Let us come together and work for a society that is just and fair. A society that unlocks the rich human potential of us all.

Let us all continue to fight for that vision. For when we do, we will live out these words: "And when this happens, and when we allow freedom to ring . . . we will be able to speed up that day when all God's children, black men and white men, Jews and Gentiles, Protestants and Catholics, will be able to join hands and sing in the words of the old Negro spiritual—'Free at last, Free at last.' Thank God Almighty, we are free at last."

'DREAM' UNLEASHES THE POWER OF KING'S HISTORIC WORDS IN '63

A book review of Bob Minzhesheimer

Forty years ago this month, my parents were planning an educational family vacation in Washington, D.C. until my father heard about plans for a massive civil rights march.

Fearing "trouble," he decided it would be safer for us to visit the battlefield at Gettysburg. The irony was lost on me for years.

Not until I read Drew Hansen's instructive slice of history, <u>The Dream: Martin Luther King Jr. and the Speech that Inspired a Nation</u>, did I realize that my father was among many who feared the March on Washington.

As Hansen recounts, the Justice Department was prepared to declare martial law if riots broke out. The Army told the FBI that it had 17,000 combat-ready troops nearby. On the eve of the march, alcohol sales were banned in Washington, prompting Malcolm X to joke, "No firewater for the Indians tomorrow."

Members of Congress told their female employees to stay home and lock the doors because the streets wouldn't be safe. The Catholic archbishop ordered nuns to stay inside.

But on August 28, 1963, about 250,000 people peacefully marched to the Lincoln Memorial where King, the final speaker, delivered his 17-minute "I Have a Dram" speech, one of the most famous in American history.

Hansen, 30, a lawyer in Seattle, wasn't even alive then. But as a student at Yale Law School he studied civil rights, and as a Rhodes Scholar at Oxford he studied theology—a perfect background to offer a new perspective on what King said that day, how he said it, and what it has come to mean.

Hansen places the march in context. He notes that in 1963 many Southern states operated segregated schools in open defiance of the Supreme Court. He writes, "Not a single black child in South Carolina, Alabama, or Mississippi attended an integrated school during the 1962-63 school year." Similarly, many Southern counties barred blacks from voting. Panola County, Mississippi had 7,250 blacks of voting age. The only black voter was 92 and had registered in 1892, during Reconstruction.

Hansen traces King's rapid rise within the civil rights movement but notes he was given the final speaking slot in part because other speakers thought the TV crews would be gone by then to process their film for the evening news.

The heart of the book is the speech itself; how King followed his prepared remarks, about the need for civil rights, for 10 minutes, then improvised the rest, a vision of an end to racism—the part that is remembered and recited.

Hansen devotes 15 pages to a side-by-side comparison between the speech King prepared and the one he delivered. He concludes, "Had King not decided to leave his written text, it is doubtful that his speech at the march would be remembered at all."

For the first time, a national audience saw a "pulpit performance that those active in the civil rights movement could see several times a year," Hansen writes. "King transformed a political rally into a vast congregation." He prepared a formal address "but ended up reaching a sermon."

And in it, he delivered a provocative promise: "Not only would children of all races live together, but this racial brotherhood was something God demanded."

The most intriguing part of the book deals with how little the speech was cited until King was assassinated five years later. During King's lifetime, most politicians wouldn't quote the speech. Now they all do.

Hansen says those who focus just on King's dream limit his legacy to problems that are settled. Jim Crow segregation is not the moral issue it was in 1963.

Hansen finds no similar consensus on questions that preoccupied King at the end of his life: residential segregation, inequalities in education and poverty. It's easier, he writes, to ignore King's speeches on these issues than to "admit that King would have been dissatisfied with the unfinished state of his crusades."

But Hansen ends on an optimistic note: "At the very lest, reflecting on the "I Have a Dream" speech should be an opportunity to be grateful for the astonishing transformation of America that the freedom movement wrought. In just under a decade, the civil rights movement brought down a system for segregation that had stood essentially unaltered since Reconstruction. King's dreams of an America free from racial discrimination are still some distance away, but it is astounding how far the nation has come since the hot August day in 1963."

AUTHORS BIOGRAPHY

The author began his career in higher education when he was appointed as an Instructor of Business at Alcorn State University immediately upon his graduation from that college. He received specialized training to prepare him for a career as a college/ university business officer. His career began at Tuskegee University in Alabama where he served with distinction for seventeen years.

During his tenure there he earned an MBA at Indiana University and the doctorate in higher education administration and finance at Auburn University. He has subsequently engaged in further advanced study at the University of Michigan, Princeton University, and Harvard University, St. Mary's Seminary, and most recently he participated in the Oxford Round Table at Oxford University.

He holds degrees from Alcorn State University, Indiana University and Auburn University. He holds two theological degrees and was awarded the honorary doctor of humanities degree from Dallas Baptist University.

Following his service at Tuskegee University he served as the Vice President for Finance and Management at Morgan State University (Maryland), President of Schenectady County Community College (New York), President of Bishop College in

Dallas, and he has served as the President of El Centro College in Dallas for twenty years.

He is a retired Lieutenant Colonel in the U.S. Army Reserve Medical Services Corps. He is an ordained Baptist minister has served as an associate pastor in New York, Mississippi, and Dallas, Texas. He served as the interim pastor of the St. John Missionary Baptist Church in Dallas for a period of approximately three years, and is currently the Associate Pastor for Development for the Concord Baptist Church in Dallas.

He has a long period of service as a teacher and preacher. He served on the faculty of the Congress of Christian Education for the Empire State Baptist Convention in New York, and on the faculty of the Northwest District Association of Christian Education, and the Baptist Missionary and Education Convention of Texas' State Congress of Christian Education. He is a Certified Dean by the National Baptist Convention, U.S.A., Inc.

He served as the Associate Minister for Christian Education and assistant to the Senior Pastor at the historic St. John Missionary Baptist Church of Dallas under the late Dr. Manuel L. Scott, Sr. for a period of twelve years.
As the Associate Pastor for Development for the Concord Missionary Baptist Church he supports the Senior Pastor and staff in the development of economic and public service initiatives for the church.

He has a distinguished record of public service and his areas of interest include education, religion, human services and business.

He has served on the graduate faculty of Dallas Baptist University since 1987 and holds the rank of Distinguished Adjunct Professor. In 2003 he was selected as the <u>John W. Turner Outstanding Adjunct Faculty Member</u> for the College of Business at the university.

He has received numerous awards for his service in education, religion, and public service. Notable among the awards is the awarding of the honorary doctor of humanities degree from Dallas Baptist University and election to the Alumni Hall of Honor of the Indiana University Graduate School of Business. He has held two presidential appointments and presently serves on the Board of Directors of the National Endowment for the Humanities, following his nomination by the President and confirmation by the U.S. Senate.

He is a nationally recognized public speaker and is a Distinguished Toastmaster. He has published sermons, speeches, monographs, in-service training manuals, and has a wide library of sermon tapes. He has preached, lectured, and taught in more than thirty states and internationally. He is the author of ten published books and eight monographs of sermons and Christian education training study guides.

In July 2005 he was one of forty-three international educators invited to participate in the <u>Oxford Round Table</u> at the historic Oxford University in England.

In May 2006 after having served as President of El Centro College for twenty years, he was appointed as Chancellor of the seven-college Dallas County Community College District. As the sixth chancellor, he is the first African-American Chancellor of the largest community college in Texas, enrolling over 100,000 students each academic term.

In 2011 he was the recipient of the Russell Perry Servant Leadership Award from Dallas Baptist University, the highest award in Dallas for a servant leader. He was the first African American recipient of that distinguished award.

He and his wife have been married for fifty-two years and they are the parents of a daughter and son, and have two granddaughters. Their daughter is an assistant vice president with J.P. Morgan Chase Bank in Dallas and their son is the chief executive officer of the Alameda County Hospital District in Oakland, California.